AF225296

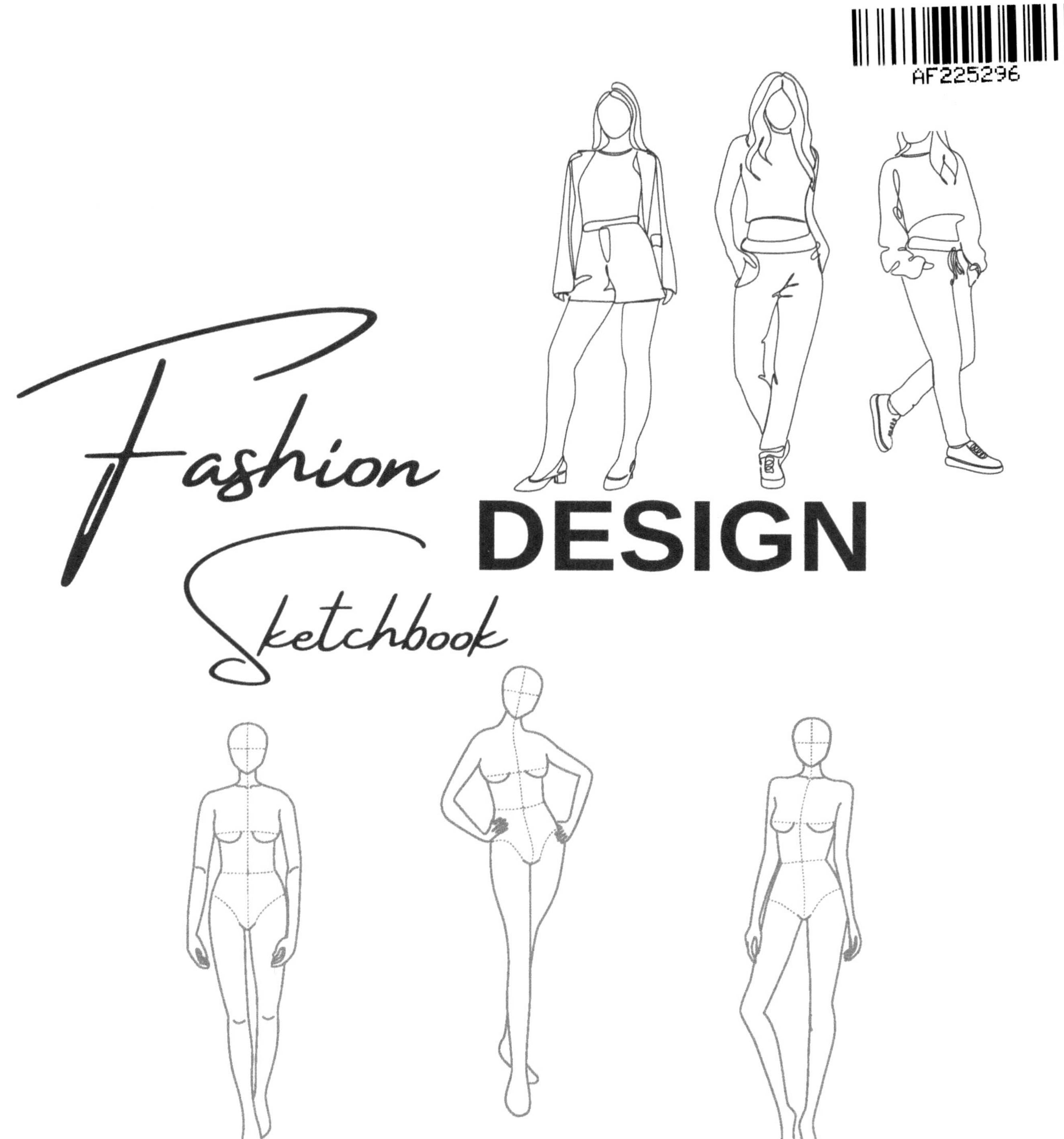

Fashion DESIGN Sketchbook

FEMALE FIGURE TEMPLATES

From Beginner to Advanced

Niky Jadesson

© Copyright 2025 – Niky Jadesson
All rights reserved.

No part of this book may be reproduced, stored in a retrieval system, or transmitted in any form or by any means – electronic, mechanical, photocopying, recording, or otherwise – without prior written permission of the author or publisher.

Legal Notice:
This publication is protected by copyright law. It is intended for personal, educational, and non-commercial use only. Copying, modifying, selling, or distributing any portion of this book without written consent is strictly prohibited.

Disclaimer:
This sketchbook is created for educational and creative practice purposes. While every effort has been made to provide accurate and helpful information, the author and publisher make no guarantees regarding results or outcomes. The material presented is general in nature and should not be considered professional advice. The reader is encouraged to exercise independent judgment. The author and publisher disclaim any liability arising from the use of this book.

Thank you for respecting the rights of the creator!

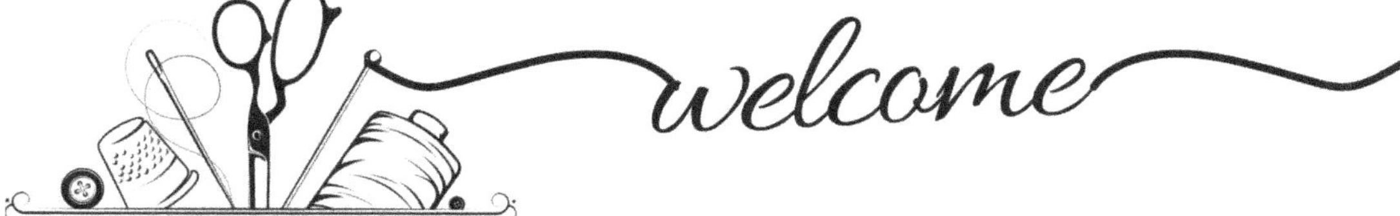

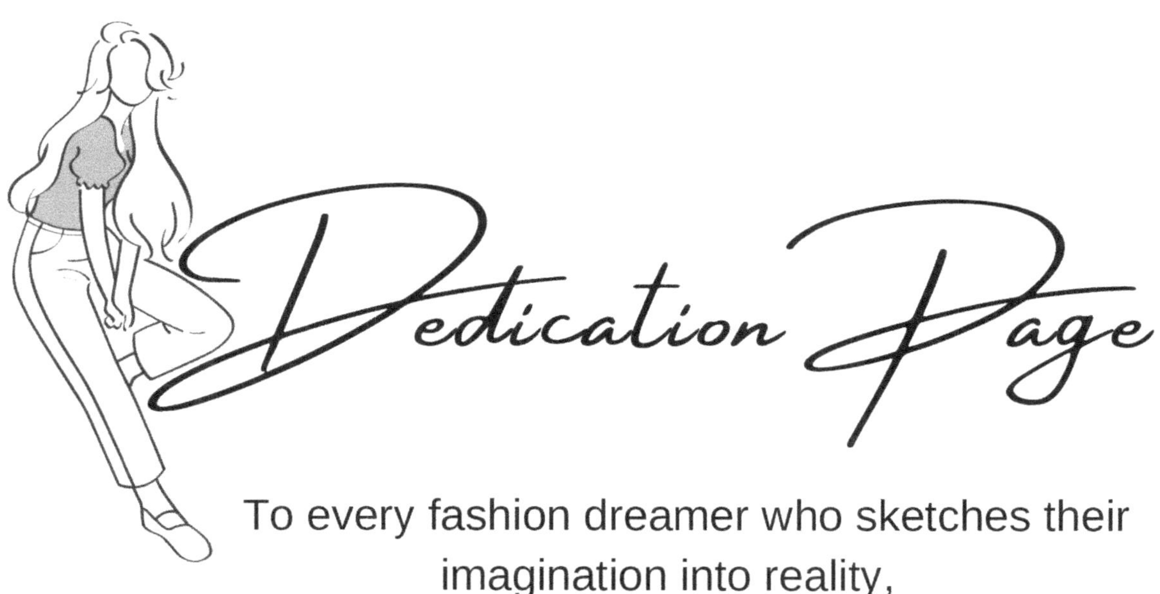

Dedication Page

To every fashion dreamer who sketches their imagination into reality,

This book was created for you – to explore, to practice, and to design freely.

May each page encourage your creativity, shape your skills, and remind you that every line you draw brings your vision closer to life.

And to the mentors, friends, and loved ones who inspire this journey – thank you for being part of the art.

With love and passion,

Niky Jadesson

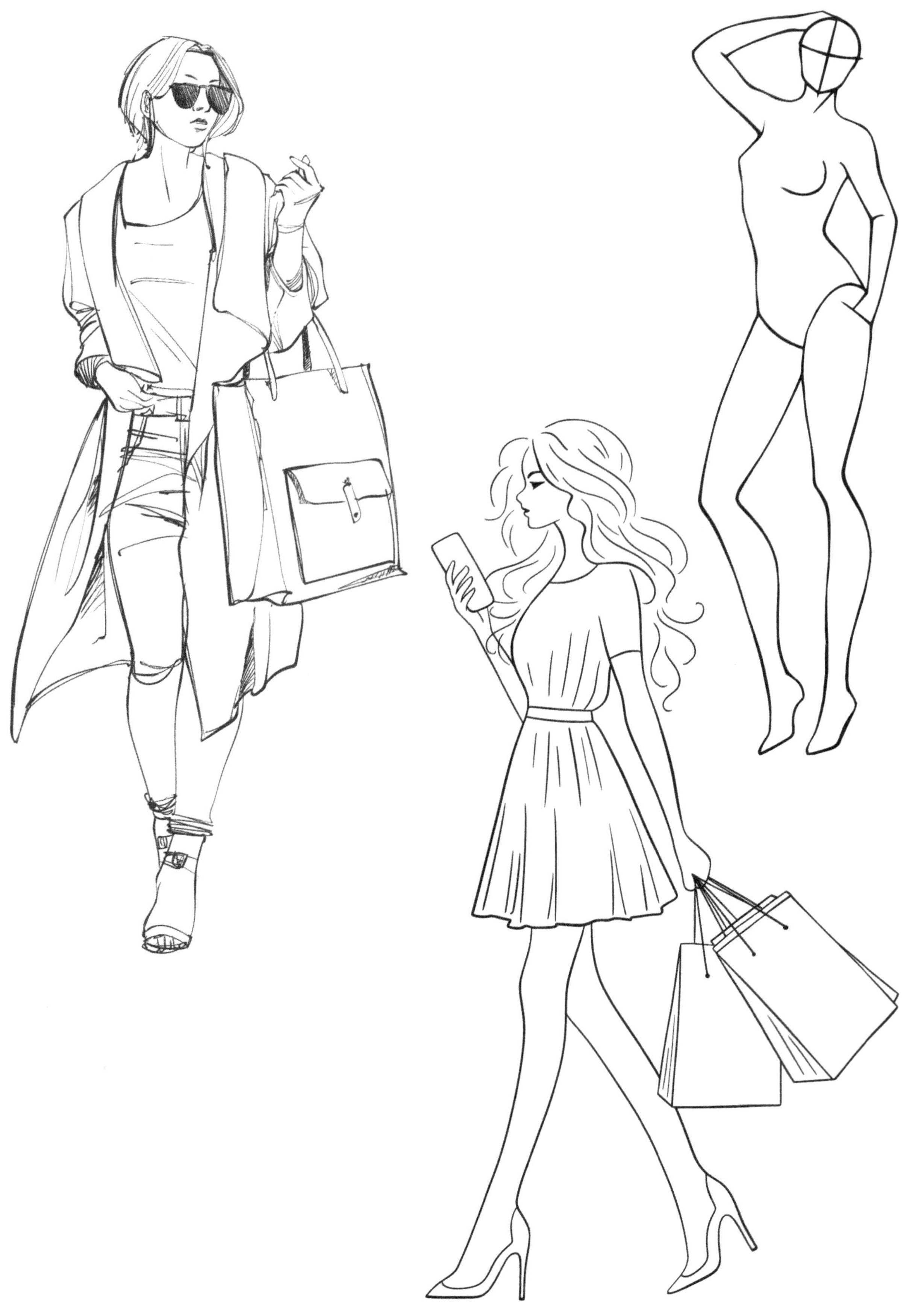

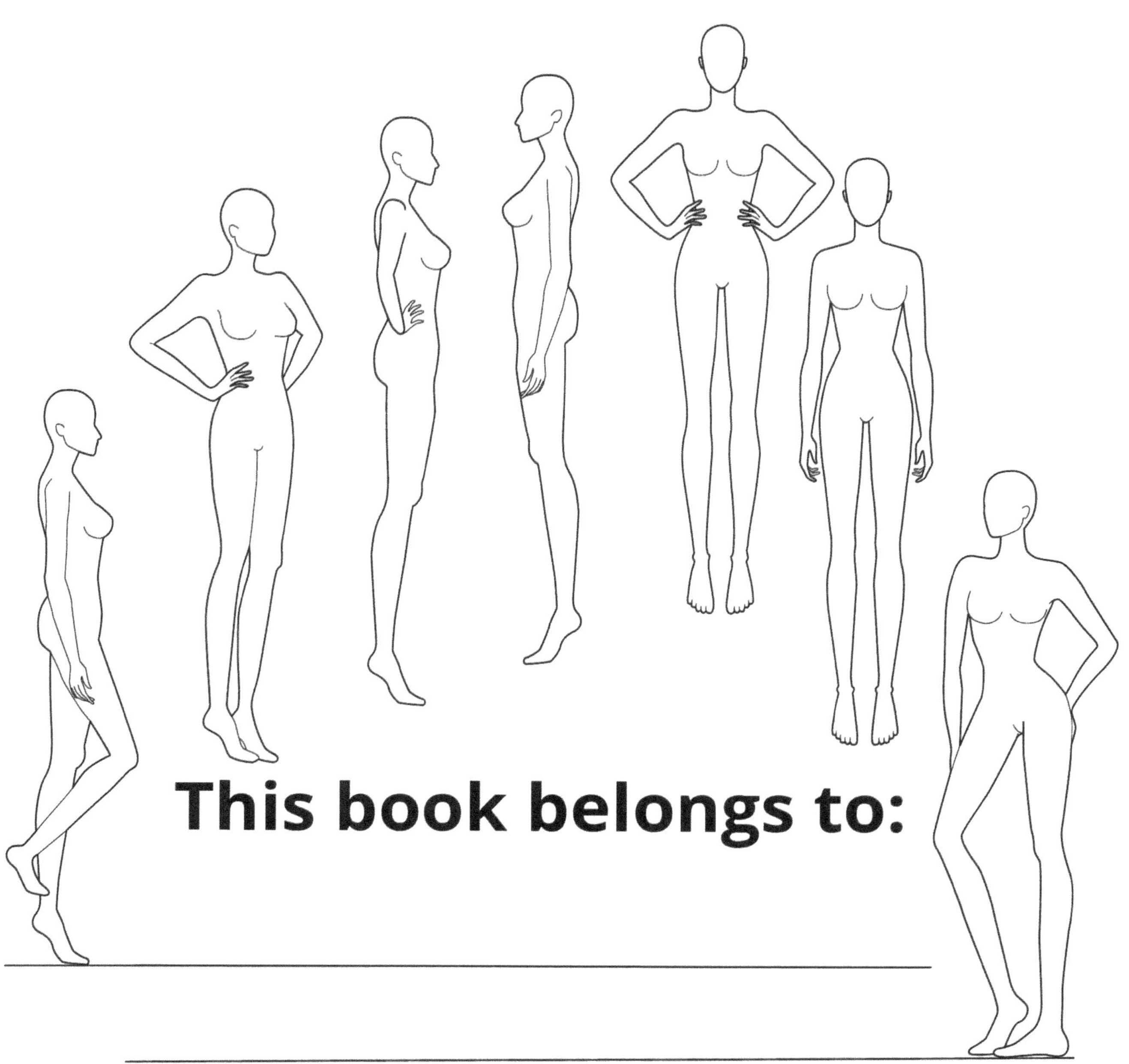

This book belongs to:

(your name)

Niky Jadesson

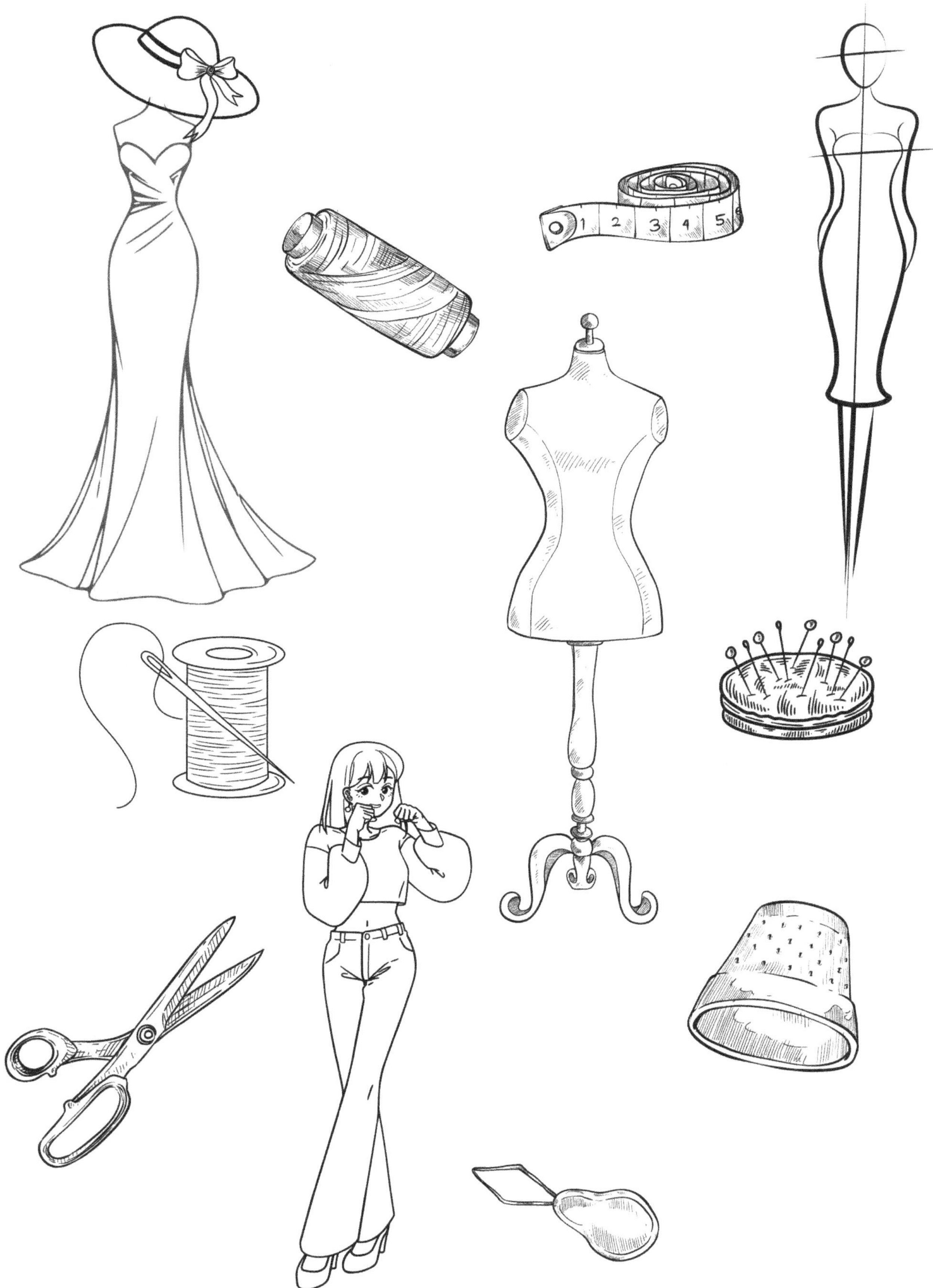

Dear friend,

Thank you so much for choosing this sketchbook! I hope it inspires you to sketch, experiment, and enjoy the art of fashion design. Each page is an invitation to bring your creative ideas to life.

If you'd like to stay updated on future books or share your feedback, I'd love to hear from you. Just search for "**Niky Jadesson Books**" online.

Your support means the world. If this book brings value to you, leaving a short review helps other readers discover it and supports independent publishing.

With gratitude,

Niky Jadesson

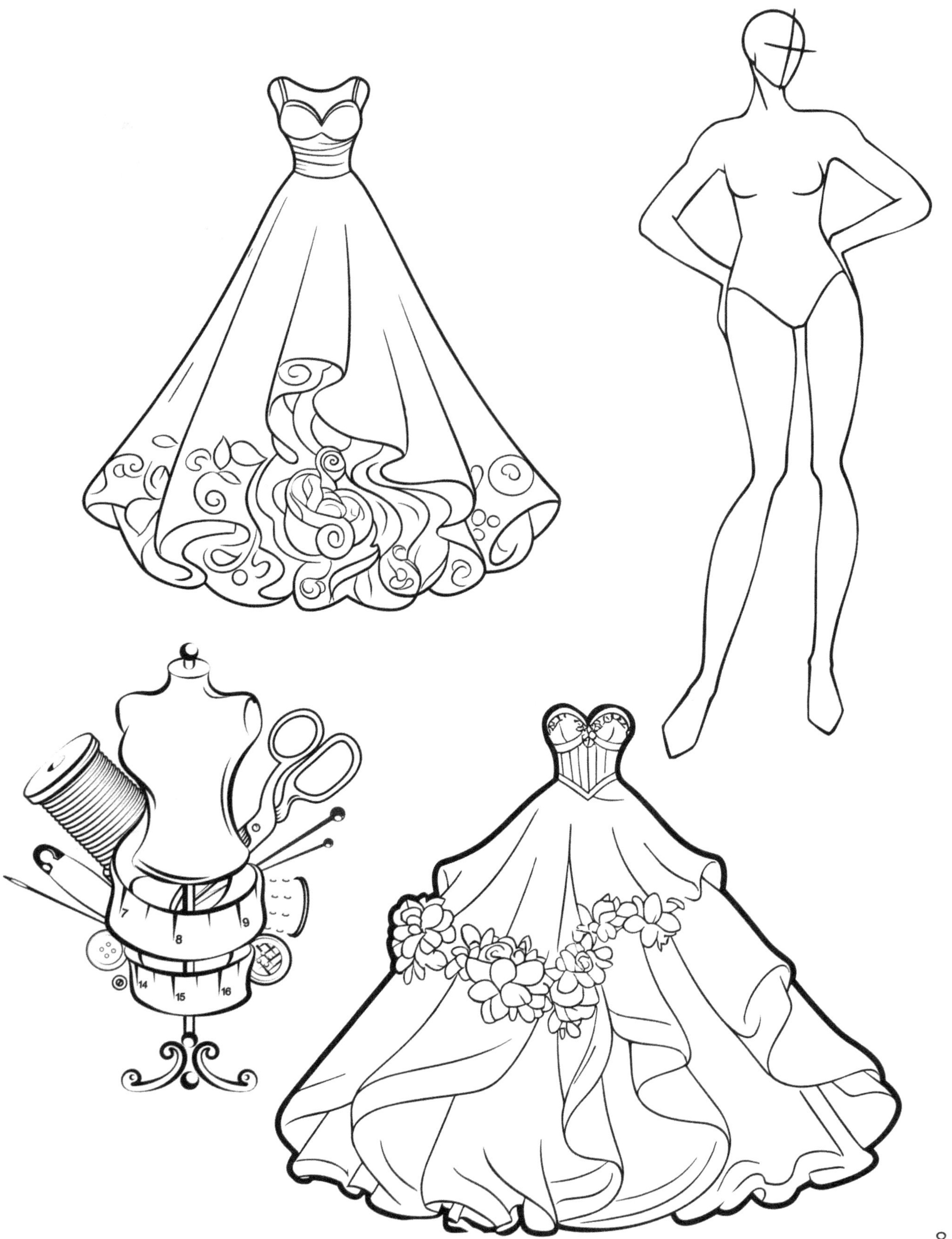

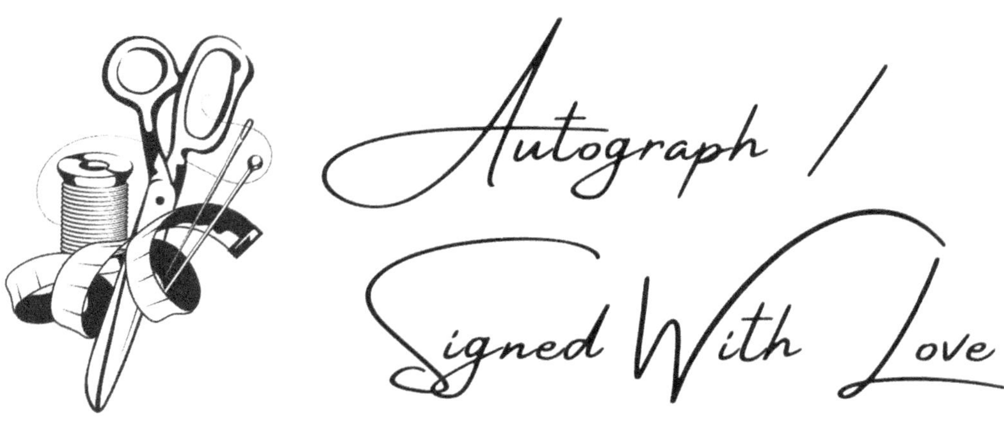

Dear _______________________,

This sketchbook is for you – to design, to create, and to celebrate your unique vision.

May it remind you that every line you draw is a step toward mastering your art.

With all my heart,

____

(Signature)

Date: _______________

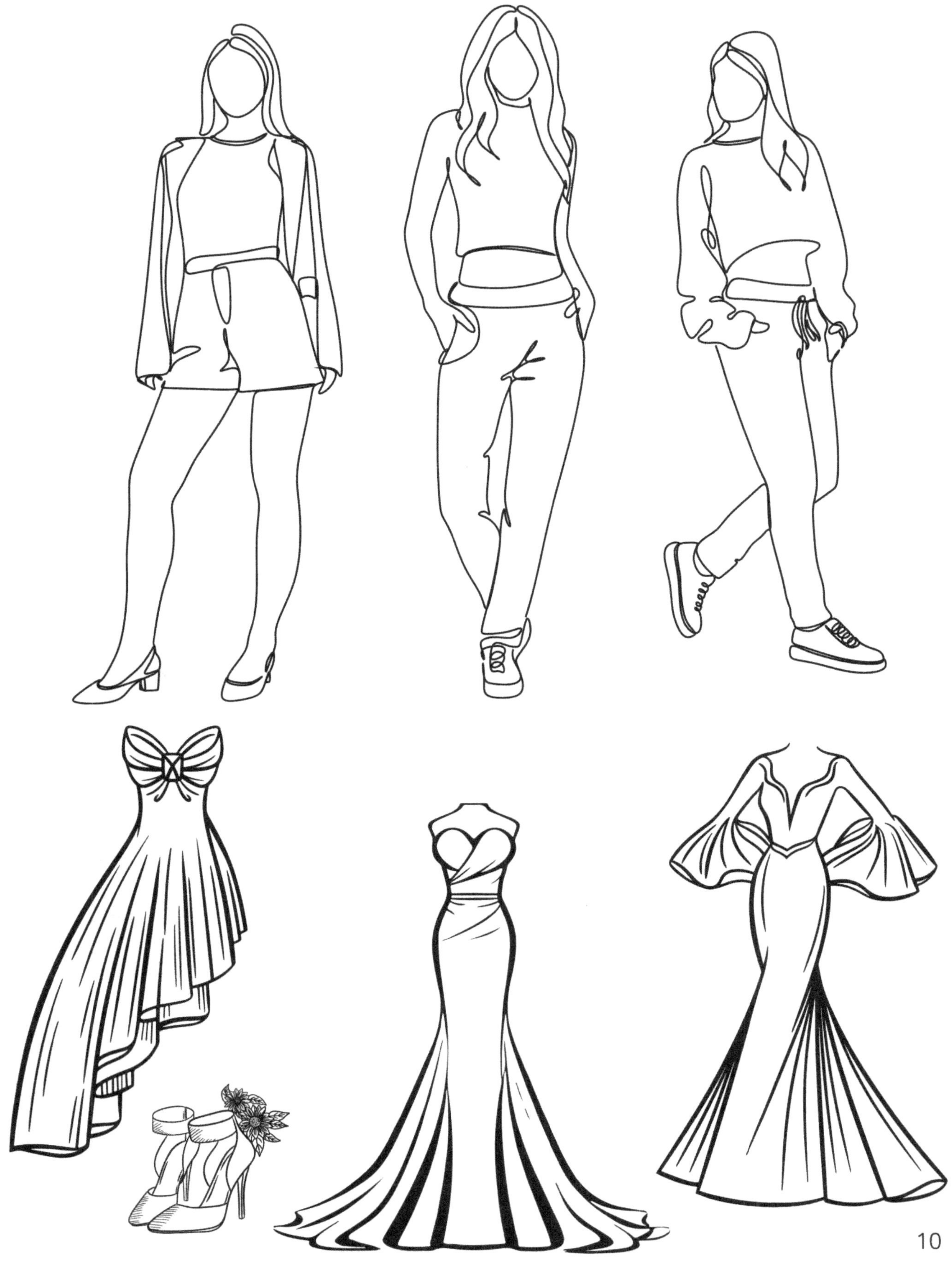

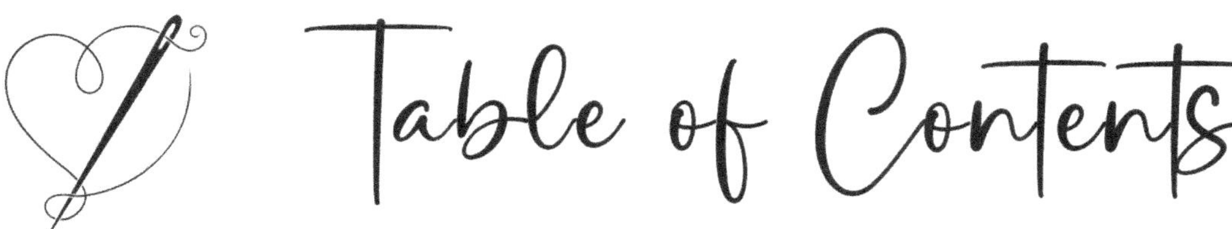

Table of Contents

Part I – Intro Pages

Part II – Education & Fundamentals 21

Table of Contents

★ ***Note:*** *The Body Templates – Female Silhouettes and practice pages are intentionally repeated across multiple sets to support structured learning, progressive creativity, and design variety.*

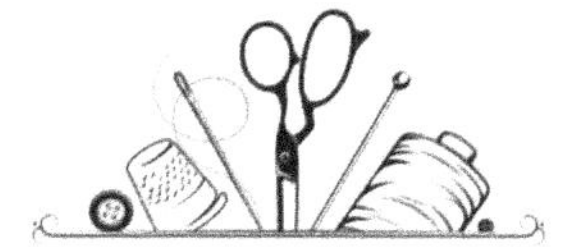

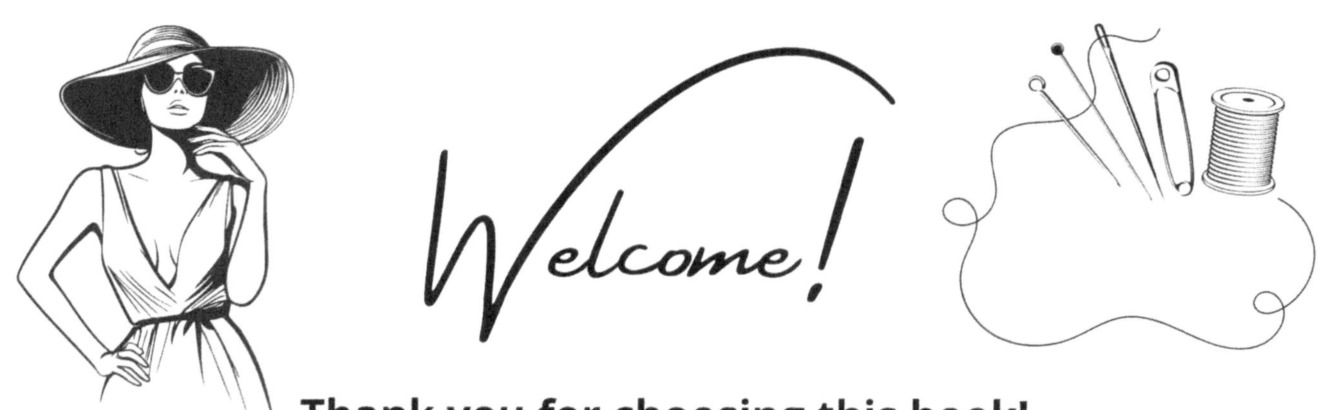

Welcome!

Thank you for choosing this book!

Fashion is more than clothes and trends – it is a language of self-expression. Every sketch is a story, and every design is a vision of who we are or who we want to become.

This sketchbook was created to help you explore, experiment, and refine your skills while bringing your fashion ideas to life.

Take your time, try out different silhouettes, fabrics, and styles, and most importantly – enjoy the process.

Whether you're a beginner just starting to sketch or already on your creative path, this is your space to grow and shine.

We're honored to be part of your journey.
Happy designing!

Niky Jadesson

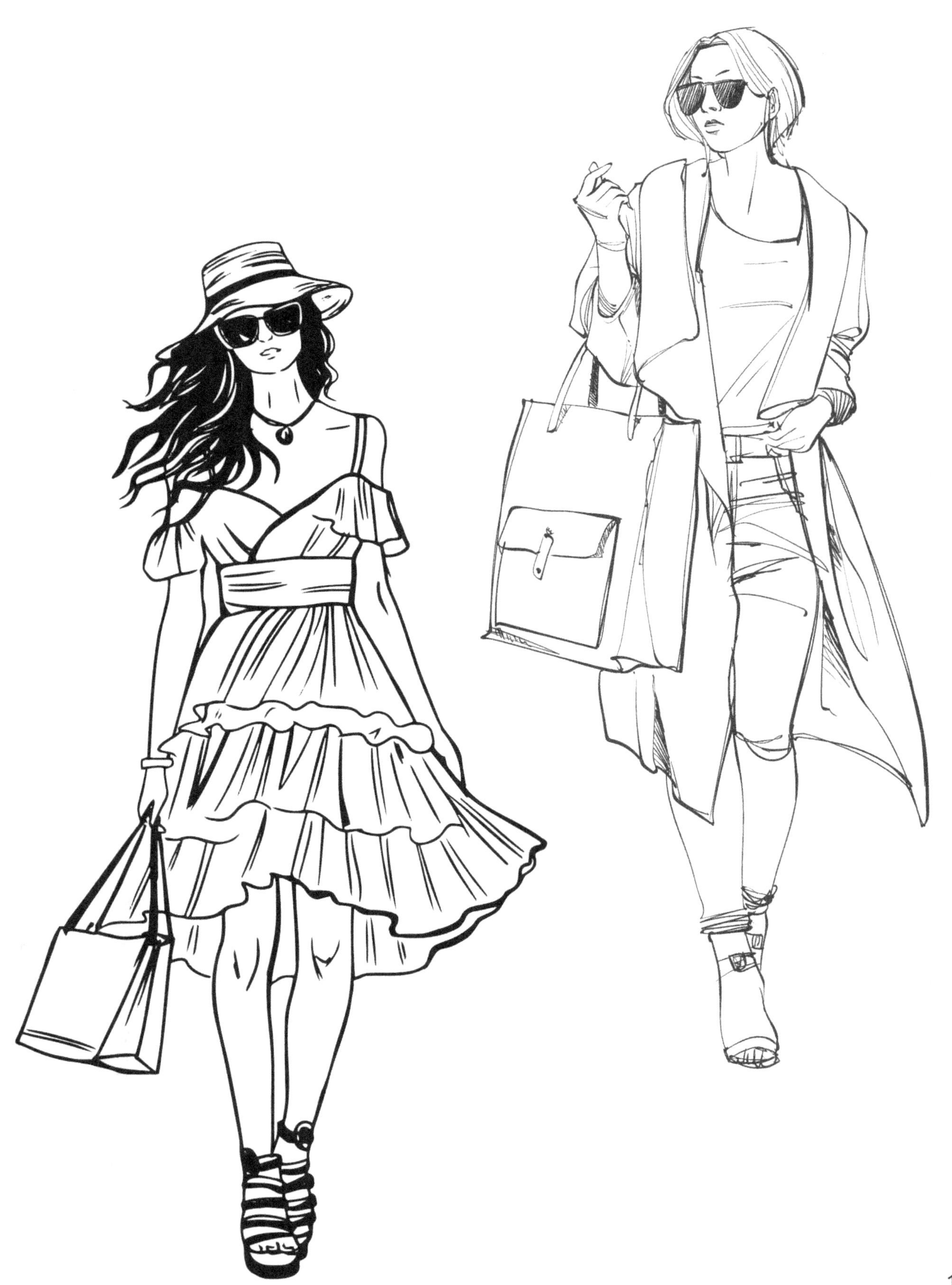

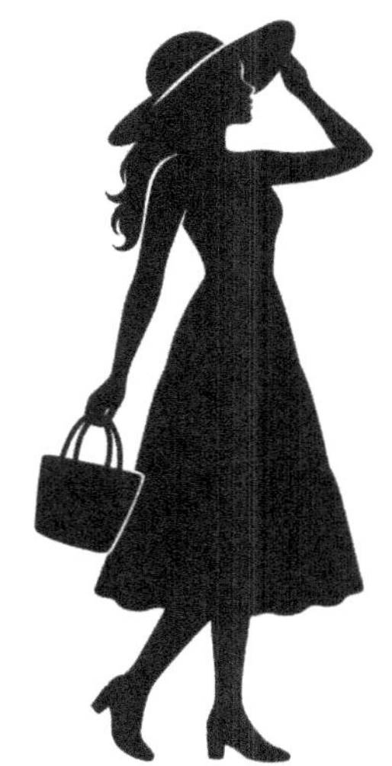

Author's Preface

Dear Reader,

Welcome to this creative journey into the world of fashion design.

This book was written with one purpose in mind: to give you a space where learning meets practice, and where every page can spark new inspiration.

Inside, you'll find both guidance and freedom.
Guidance, through explanations of fashion fundamentals, silhouettes, fabrics, and professional tips.
Freedom, through body templates, outfit inspirations, and practice pages – where your imagination has no limits.

Fashion is personal. It is about identity, creativity, and confidence.
I hope these pages inspire you to experiment, to enjoy the process, and to see fashion as the art form it truly is.

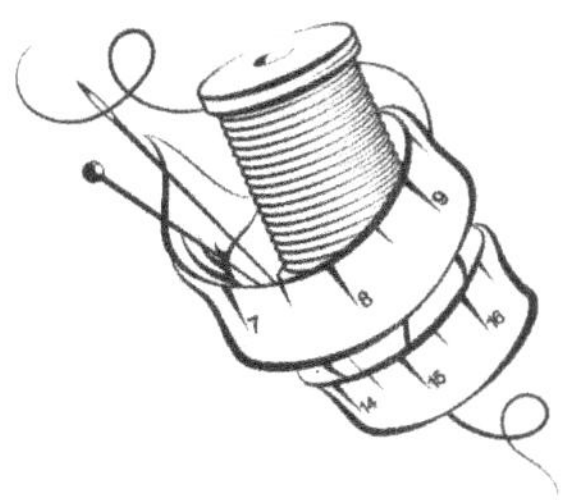

With passion and gratitude,
Niky Jadesson

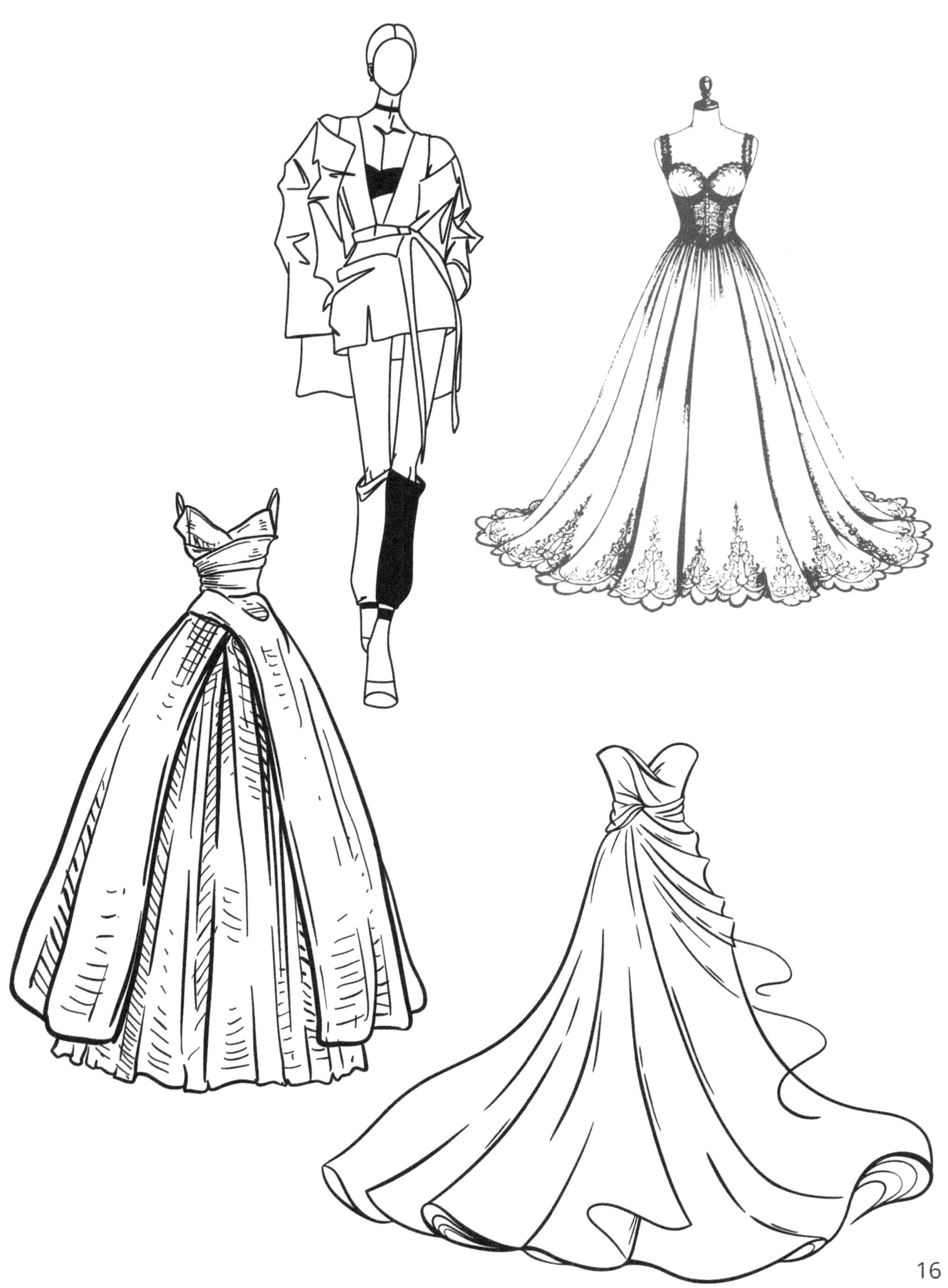

How to Use This Sketchbook

This sketchbook is designed to be both practical and creative.

It gives you space to explore outfit ideas, practice sketching techniques, and reflect on your personal style.

Here are a few tips to get the most out of it:

- **Experiment Freely** – Try out different silhouettes, color palettes, and fabrics.
- **Take Notes** – Use the practice guide pages to write down your ideas, inspirations, or material choices.
- **Practice on Templates** – The body figures are made to help you visualize outfits before turning them into real garments.
- **Compare & Improve** – Use the photo/inspiration pages to attach references and see how your sketches evolve.
- **Repeat & Refine** – Don't hesitate to redraw the same idea with small changes. Growth comes with repetition.

Whether you are a beginner learning step by step, or a designer sharpening your skills, this sketchbook is your personal creative studio.

My Goals & Inspirations

Fashion design is more than drawing clothes - it's about expressing identity, lifestyle, and emotions through what we create. This page is for you to reflect on your journey as a designer and to capture the goals that guide your practice.

Ask yourself:
- What kind of fashion do I want to design? (casual wear, haute couture, evening dresses, street style)
- Who inspires me the most? (designers, artists, icons, or even everyday people)
- What emotions do I want my clothes to transmit? (confidence, elegance, freedom, joy)

Write it down here:
- My design goals: ....
- My style inspirations: ....
- Fabrics or colors I want to explore: ....
- Skills I want to improve: ....

Tip*: Revisiting your goals every few months can show you how much your vision has evolved.*

Tools & Materials
for Fashion Sketching

Having the right tools doesn't mean you need expensive supplies - it's about knowing how to use them. Here are some essentials for fashion sketching, especially for women's fashion:

- **Pencils & Shading Tools** – HB for light sketching, 2B–6B for shading details like folds, ruffles, or pleats.
- **Fineliners** – For clear outlines and defining elements like lace or embroidery.
- **Markers & Colored Pencils** – Perfect for capturing fabrics: pastel tones for chiffon, metallic markers for satin, deep shades for velvet.
- **Ruler & Curves** – Use them for precise lines on skirts, trousers, or fitted bodices.
- **Digital Tools** – Tablets and software (Procreate, Photoshop, Illustrator) for clean, professional designs.
- **Fabric Swatches** – Touching real fabrics helps you understand texture and drape.

__Remember__: it's not about the price of the tool, but about how you use it to tell your story.

Tips
for Getting Started

Starting can feel overwhelming, but the secret is consistency. Here are some practical tips:

- **Start Simple** – Focus on dresses, tops, and skirts before moving to layered outfits.
- **Observe & Analyze** – Study how real garments fit on women: how a dress hugs the body, how a blouse drapes at the shoulders.
- **Practice Silhouettes** – Work with different body shapes: hourglass, A-line, empire, bodycon.
- **Experiment with Colors** – Try contrasting palettes, seasonal tones, or even monochrome designs.
- **Don't Chase Perfection** – The first sketches are about freedom, not flawlessness.

Every successful designer started with imperfect sketches. Progress comes from showing up every day, not from waiting for the "perfect" design.

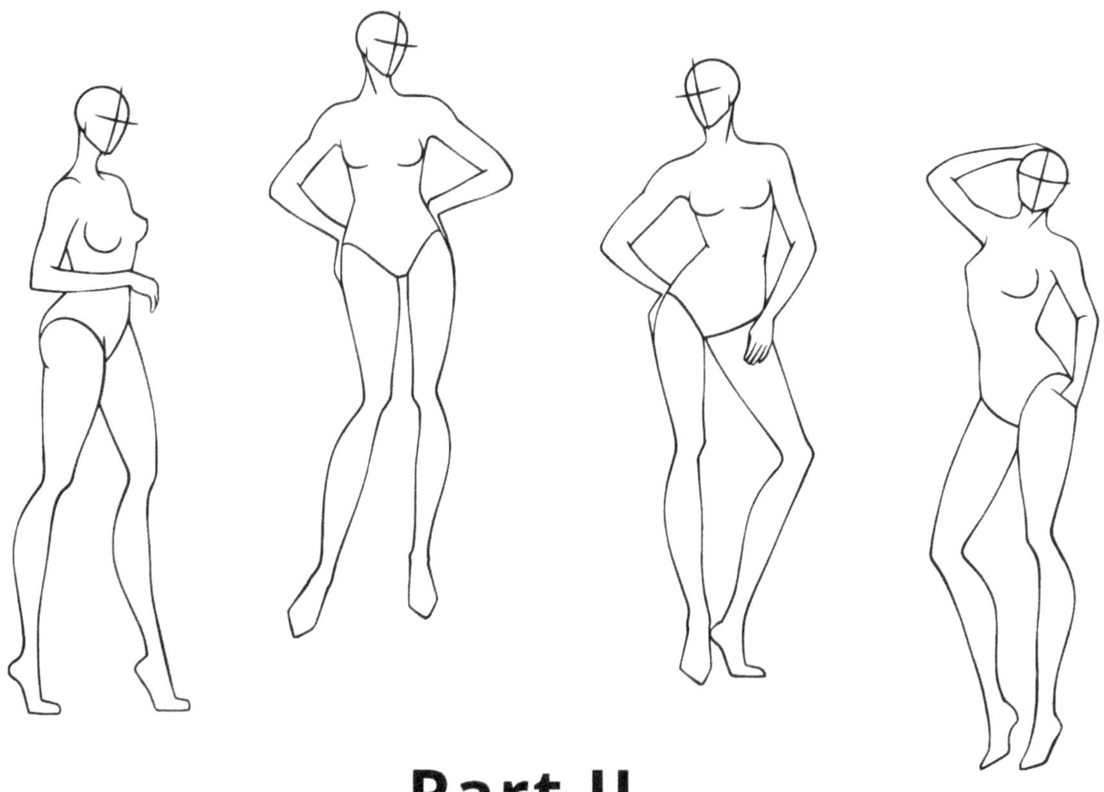

Part II
– Education & Fundamentals

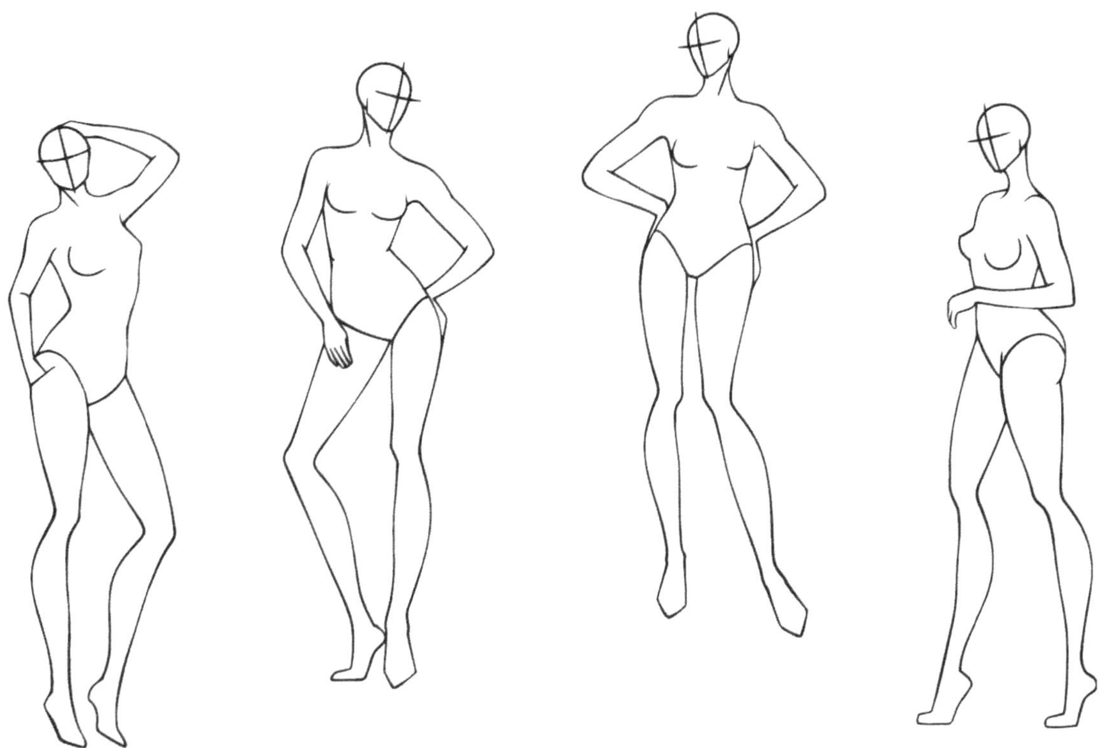

A Short History of Women's Fashion
– *From Classic Eras to Modern Styles*

Fashion has always reflected culture and identity. Women's fashion, in particular, has shifted with society's values, new materials, and the role of women through history.

- **Ancient Civilizations** – Women wore flowing garments made from linen or wool, often draped around the body. Jewelry and belts added individuality. Clothing was practical but still elegant.
- **Medieval & Renaissance Eras** – Dresses became layered and structured, showing status and wealth. Fabrics like velvet and brocade were reserved for the upper classes, while detailed embroidery turned clothing into art.
- **18th & 19th Centuries** – Silhouettes varied widely: from the wide skirts of the Rococo era to the cinched waists and bustles of the Victorian period. Fashion often emphasized modesty and social rank.
- **20th Century** – Rapid change defined the century. The early decades introduced simpler dresses, while mid-century fashion celebrated femininity with defined waists and skirts. Later decades embraced individuality, bold shapes, and modern fabrics.
- **Today** – Women's fashion celebrates diversity. Styles range from minimalist everyday looks to avant-garde experimental designs. Comfort, sustainability, and inclusivity are as important as elegance.

Every fashion era tells a story. Now it's your turn to shape the next one through your sketches.

Female Silhouettes Through Time
– *Hourglass, A-Line, Empire, Bodycon*

The silhouette is the foundation of every design-it defines shape, proportion, and first impression.

- **Hourglass** – A narrow waist with balanced bust and hips. Classic, feminine, and versatile.
- **A-Line** – Fitted at the top, flaring gradually toward the hem. Comfortable and flattering for many body types.
- **Empire Waist** – High waistline under the bust with a flowing skirt. Creates elegance and elongates the figure.
- **Bodycon** – Close-fitting designs that emphasize natural curves, usually made with stretch fabrics.

Silhouettes are more than shapes-they carry emotions. Hourglass silhouettes feel romantic, A-Line feels playful, Empire feels graceful, and Bodycon feels bold.

When sketching, always think: *What mood do I want this outfit to create?*

Color Theory in Women's Fashion
– Matching, Contrasts & Seasonal Palettes

Color transforms clothing from simple fabric into visual storytelling.

- **Warm vs. Cool Tones** – Warm colors (reds, oranges, yellows) suggest energy and passion. Cool tones (blues, greens, purples) convey calm and sophistication.
- **Contrast & Harmony** – Opposite colors on the color wheel create drama and boldness. Neighboring shades feel soft and harmonious.
- **Seasonal Palettes** – Designers often think of palettes as seasonal moods:
  - *Spring*: light pastels, airy and playful.
  - *Summer*: cool tones, fresh and vibrant.
  - *Autumn*: earthy shades, cozy and rich.
  - *Winter*: deep contrasts, elegant and strong.
- Psychology of Color – Light shades open up space and feel fresh. Dark shades create mystery and authority. Bright colors attract attention, while muted tones create subtlety.

Experiment by coloring the same design in three different palettes-you'll see how dramatically the mood shifts.

Fabrics & Textures for Women's Clothing
– *Lace, Satin, Denim, Tweed*

The right fabric can elevate or completely change a design.

- **Lace** – Light, delicate, perfect for layering or romantic looks.
- **Satin** – Smooth, shiny, ideal for gowns and formal wear.
- **Denim** – Strong, casual, versatile, found in everything from streetwear to high fashion.
- **Tweed** – Structured, textured, excellent for outerwear and sophisticated styles.

When designing, imagine how the fabric will move. Does it drape softly, does it hold shape, does it shimmer in the light? The texture is just as important as the cut.

Pro tip: Sketch the same outfit in two different fabrics. A tweed suit looks formal, while the same cut in denim feels relaxed.

Fashion Sketching Tools

– Pencils, Markers, Digital Options

Tools are your partners in creativity.

- **Pencils** – Great for initial outlines, shading, and details.
- **Markers** – Ideal for adding quick pops of color and experimenting with palettes.
- **Colored Pencils** – Useful for layering tones, blending, and creating soft gradients.
- **Watercolors** – Add flow and texture for dreamy, artistic sketches.
- **Digital Tools** – Tablets and software offer unlimited colors, textures, and undo options.

Don't wait for expensive tools to start. Even a simple pencil and paper can bring powerful ideas to life.

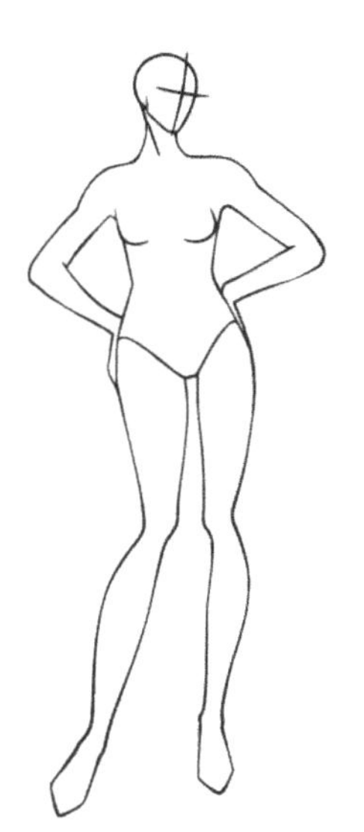
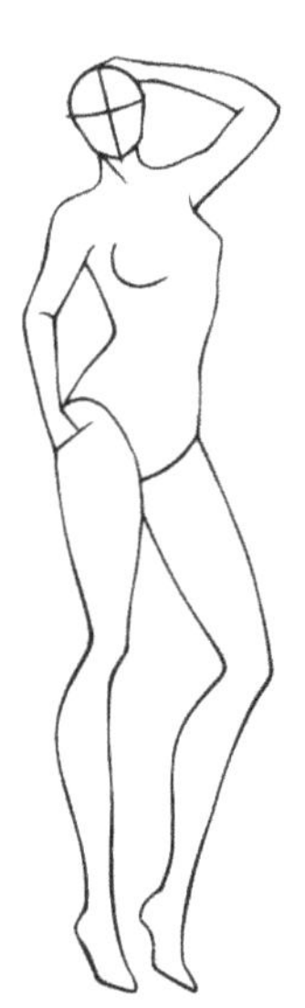
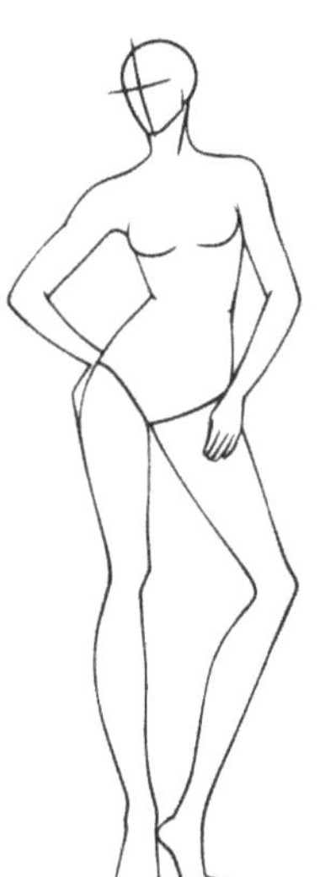
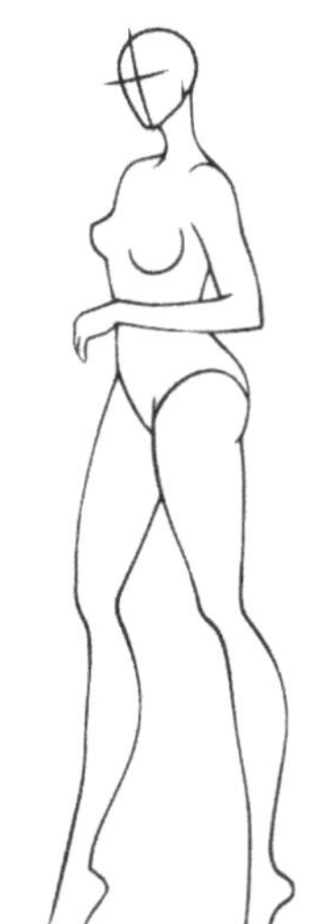

Step-by-Step:
Casual Day Outfit (Dress, Skirt, Blouse)

Everyday fashion balances comfort and style. Try this process:

1. **Base Sketch** – Start with a simple female silhouette.
2. **Outline the Garment** – Think of lightweight fabrics like cotton or linen.
3. **Add Details** – Buttons, collars, or simple accessories.
4. **Choose a Palette** – Neutrals with a pop of color often work best.
5. **Finalize Texture** – Shade to show softness or crispness.

The key is wearability. A casual design should feel easy and effortless while still stylish.

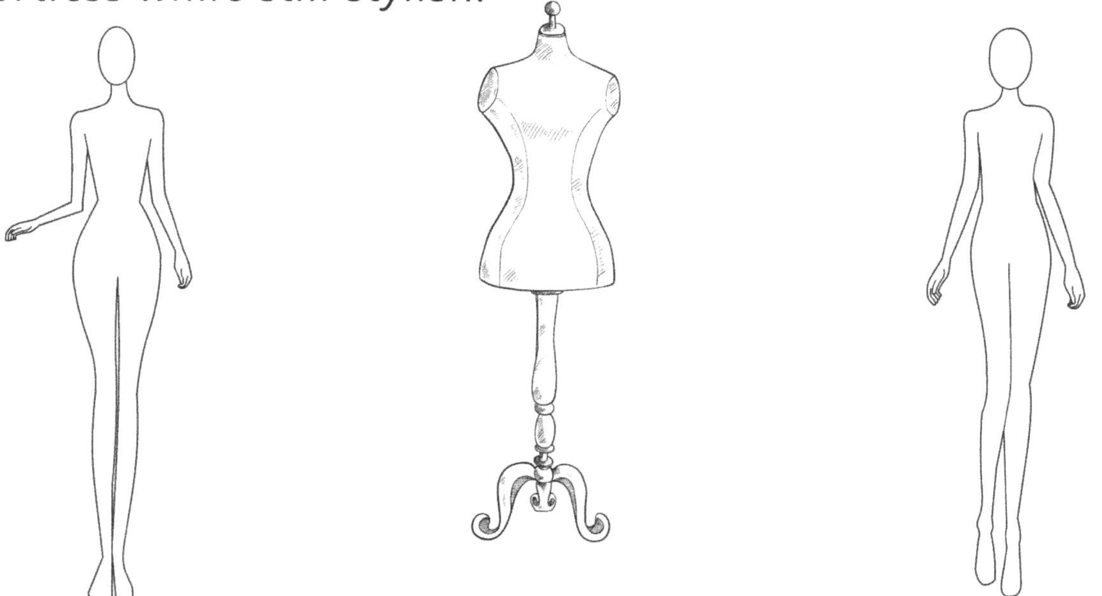

Step-by-Step:
Evening Glam Look (Cocktail & Evening Dresses)

Eveningwear is about elegance and statement. Try this flow:

1. **Choose the Silhouette** – A-Line, mermaid, or body-hugging styles.
2. **Pick Fabrics** – Shiny or flowing fabrics like satin, velvet, or chiffon.
3. **Add Design Features** – Off-shoulder cuts, open backs, high slits, or embellishments.
4. **Select Colors** – Deep jewel tones, metallics, or bold contrasts.
5. **Finalize Accessories** – Heels, jewelry, clutch.

Evening looks should make the wearer feel confident, glamorous, and unforgettable.

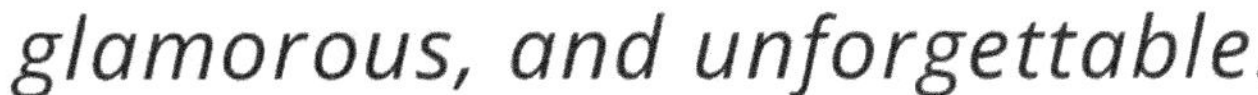

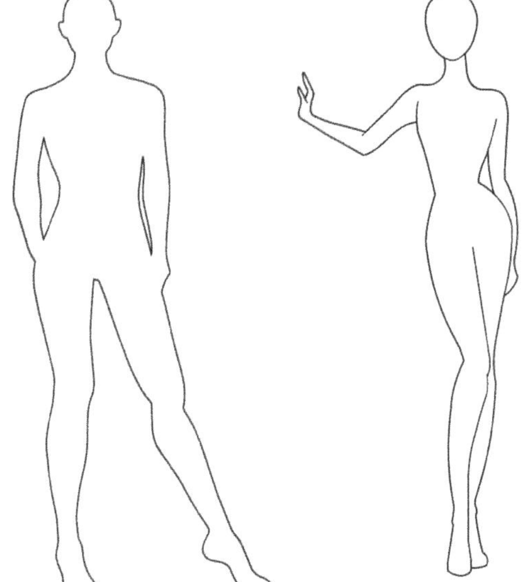

Common Design Mistakes
in Women's Fashion

(and How to Avoid Them)

Even experienced designers face challenges. Here are a few pitfalls:

- **Overcrowding the Design** – Too many details can overwhelm. Simplify where possible.
- **Ignoring Fabric Movement** – A sketch may look good, but if fabric doesn't support it, the outfit fails.
- **Color Overload** – Using too many bold colors can distract from the design. Stick to a balanced palette.
- **Proportion Problems** – A skirt too long or sleeves too short can distort the look. Always check balance.
- **Copying Trends Too Closely** – Inspiration is fine, but originality sets a designer apart.

Every mistake is an opportunity. The key is to adjust, refine, and improve.

Tips & Tricks for Women's Fashion Designers

- Always sketch multiple variations before settling on one design.
- Think of layering-outfits are more versatile when pieces can mix and match.
- Neutral palettes can be powerful; you don't always need bold colors.
- Sketch with movement-imagine how fabric drapes and flows.
- Keep notes on what inspired you. Ideas fade fast, but written details preserve them.

Designing is not just about the clothes, but the story they tell.

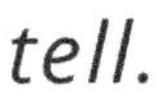

Step-by-Step Guide
to This Sketchbook

This Sketchbook is your design studio on paper. Here's how to use it:

- **Practice** – Start with basic silhouettes provided. Don't rush-focus on building confidence.
- **Experiment** – Test different fabrics, palettes, and shapes. Use colored pencils, markers, or even fabric swatches.
- **Document** – Use the notes pages to track progress, write reflections, and save inspiration.
- **Create Collections** – Think in sets of outfits that share a theme.
- **Review** – Look back at older sketches to see how much your style has evolved.

By the end of this sketchbook, you will not only have dozens of sketches but also a clear sense of your own fashion identity.

Fashion Sketching Fundamentals:
Step by Step

Fashion sketching is the foundation of every design journey. While techniques may evolve over time, following a structured process helps you create balanced and expressive sketches. Here is a simple, step-by-step approach tailored to women's fashion:

Step 1: Build the Basic Silhouette
- Start with the body proportions of the female figure.
- Sketch guidelines for shoulders, waist, hips, and legs.
- Remember that the female silhouette often emphasizes curves, so keep your lines fluid.

Step 2: Outline the Main Garment Shapes
- Add basic geometric forms to represent the main clothing pieces: dresses, skirts, blouses, or trousers.
- Think of circles for flowy skirts, rectangles for structured jackets, and ovals for softer tops.

Step 3: Add Clothing Details
- Draw in elements like collars, sleeves, cuffs, buttons, belts, or hemlines.
- Use clean lines to keep proportions accurate.

Step 4: Represent Fabrics & Textures
- Indicate fabric type through linework:
    - Light, flowing fabrics (silk, chiffon) → use long, curved lines.
    - Heavy fabrics (denim, wool) → use short, firm lines.
    - Lace or delicate textures → small, intricate detailing.

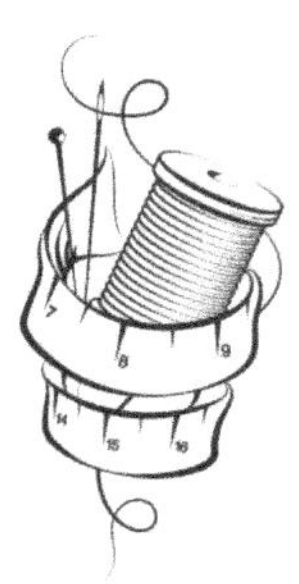

Step 5: Add Color & Shading
- Introduce a color palette: neutrals, pastels, or bold contrasts.
- Use shading to show volume, folds, and fabric depth.

Step 6: Refine & Finalize
- Go over key lines to highlight the silhouette.
- Leave room for notes: fabric ideas, color inspirations, or intended occasion.

Fashion sketching is not about perfection but about expression. These steps give you structure, but your creativity is what brings designs to life.

Mini Exercise:
Sketch the same outfit twice – once in a casual version (cotton blouse and denim skirt) and once in a formal version (silk blouse and pencil skirt). Notice how fabrics and small details change the overall look.

QUICK & EASY EVERYDAY FASHION LOOK

Let's put theory into practice with a simple, casual daytime outfit. Everyday fashion is about comfort and effortless style while still showing personality.

5 Steps to Design a Casual Day Look:

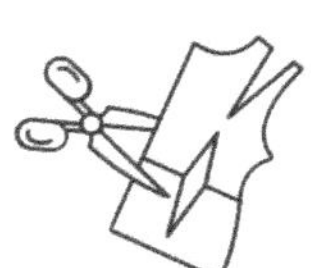

1. Draw a relaxed female silhouette.
2. Add a light blouse or fitted t-shirt as the top.
3. Complete the outfit with jeans, a skirt, or leggings.
4. Include practical footwear – sneakers, flats, or sandals.
5. Suggest small accessories like a tote bag or a bracelet.

Styling Notes:

- Everyday fashion often relies on neutral tones with one or two accent colors.
- Comfort is key – fabrics like cotton or jersey work well.
- Layering (a light jacket, a scarf, or a cardigan) can instantly elevate a casual look.

Why Practice This?

Casual looks may appear simple, but they teach balance and proportion. They are also a great way to practice sketching movement and fluidity since casual outfits are rarely rigid.

Reflection Prompt:

- What colors best represent your personal "everyday" style?
- How would this look change if you replaced sneakers with heels or boots?

Use this page to sketch your own quick outfit idea. Don't focus on details too much-let your hand move freely and enjoy the process.

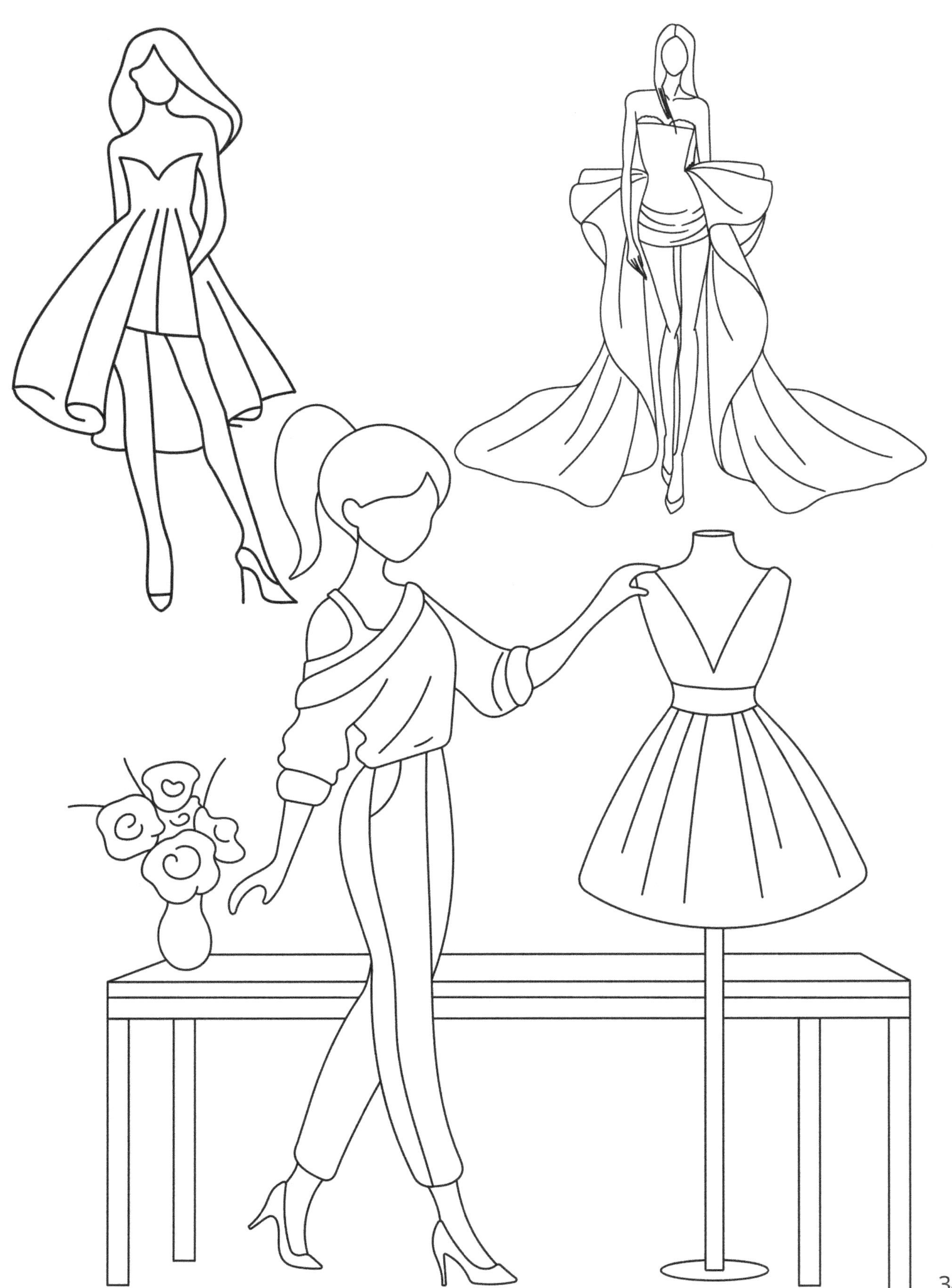

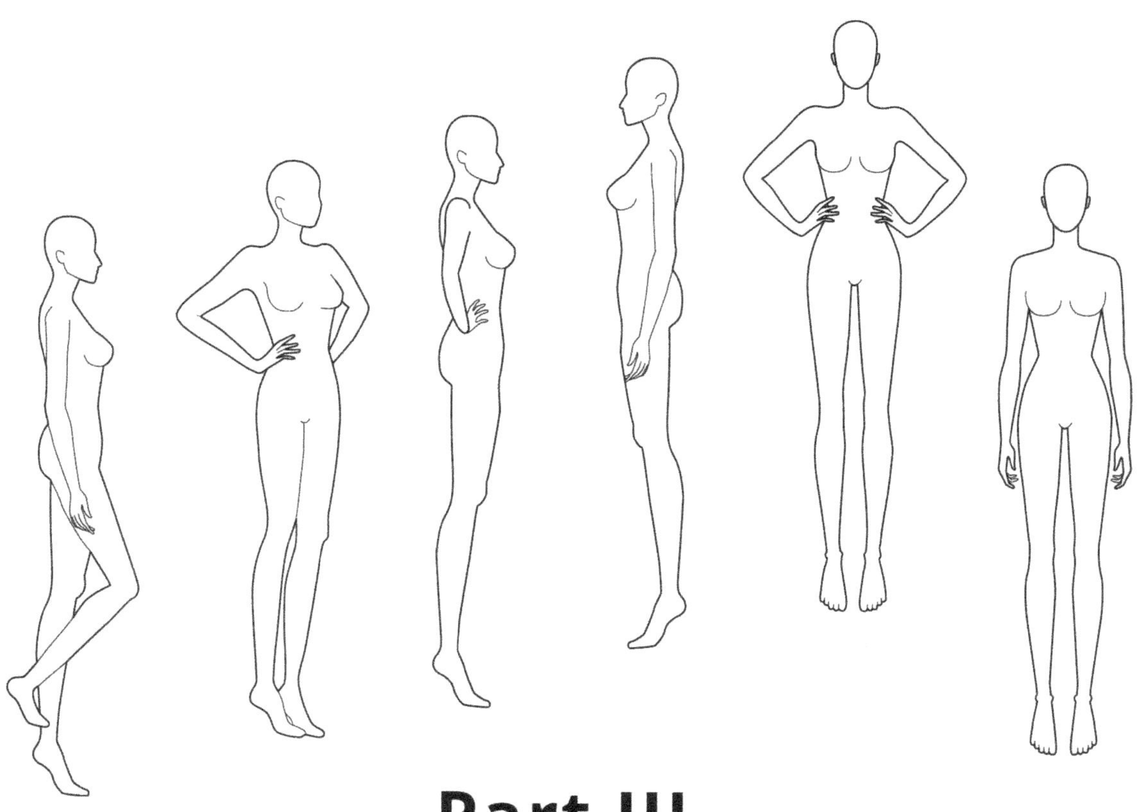

Part III
– Sketchbook & Practice

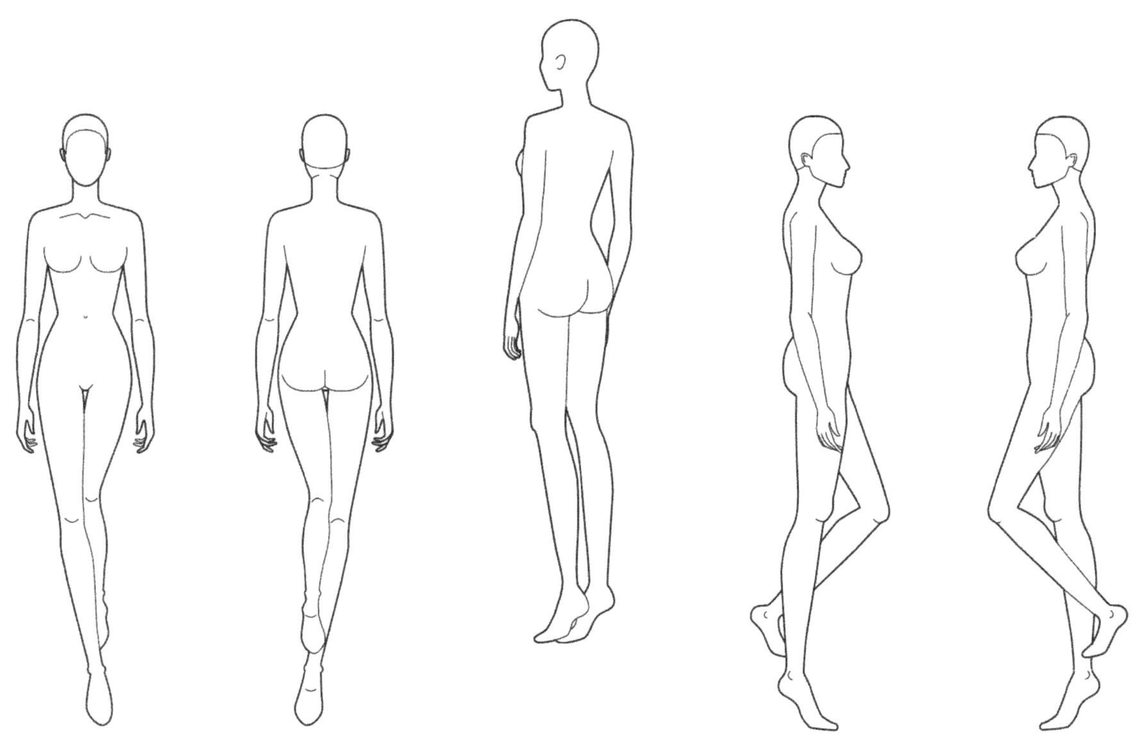

Fashion Practice Guide & Notes

Fashion design is about exploration, not perfection. Use this page to try something bold-even if it feels outside your comfort zone. Mistakes are part of growth, and every sketch teaches you something new.

How to Use This Page:
- Experiment with proportions you don't usually draw.
- Add layers to see how fabrics interact.
- Use notes to describe movement or flow in the outfit.

Reflection & Notes:
- What new technique did I try today?
- Did the design feel balanced?
- Which detail could I refine in the next sketch?

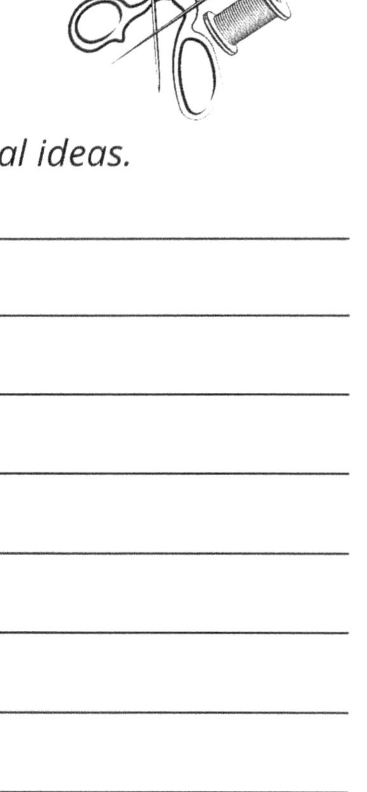

Pro Tip: *Bold experiments often lead to your most original ideas.*

Outfit Inspiration: Streetwear

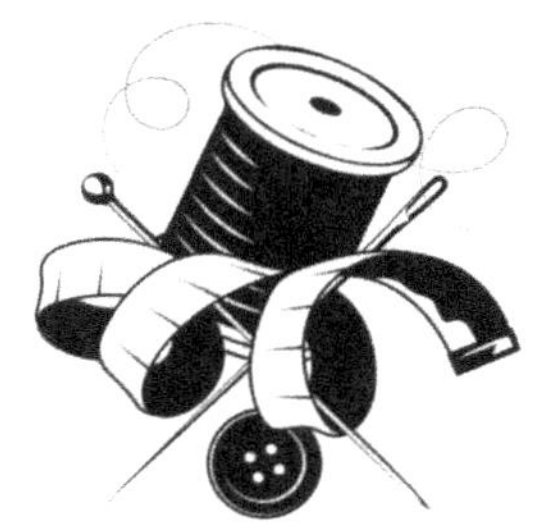

The Power of Layering

Streetwear thrives on layers – they allow creativity, versatility, and endless combinations. Start with a simple base such as a fitted tank top and leggings, then build up with oversized shirts, bomber jackets, or denim vests. Add a hoodie under a trench coat, or a plaid shirt tied at the waist. Each new layer transforms the silhouette and adds depth.

Experiment with contrasts: soft fabrics under structured jackets, or bold prints layered over neutral basics. Layering is also practical – it makes an outfit adaptable to different weathers and moods.

Try this: sketch a look starting with a crop top and cargo pants, then add a zip-up hoodie, an oversized jacket, and sneakers. Notice how each layer changes the vibe.

Trends

Inspiration

Textiles

Notes

Details

Swatches

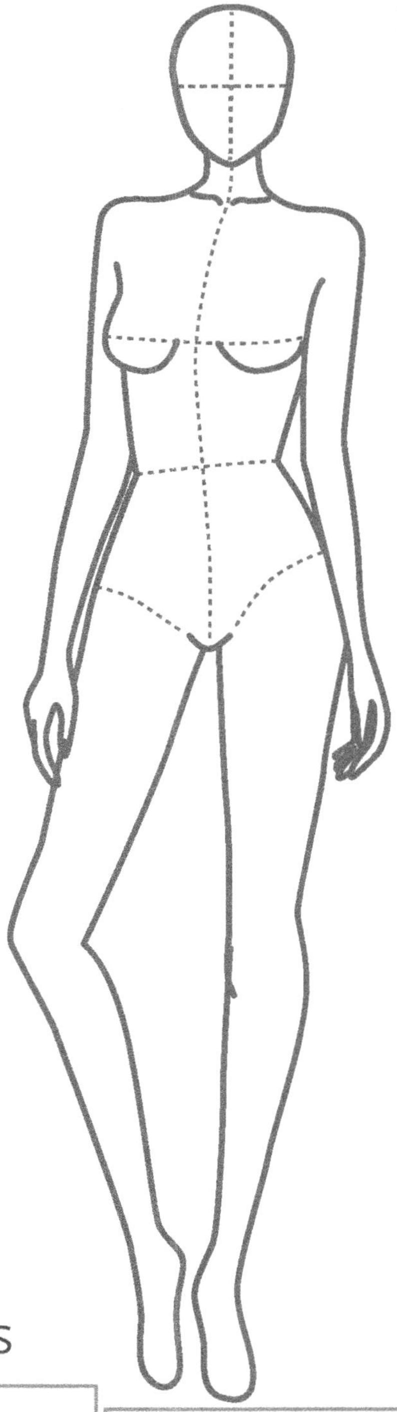

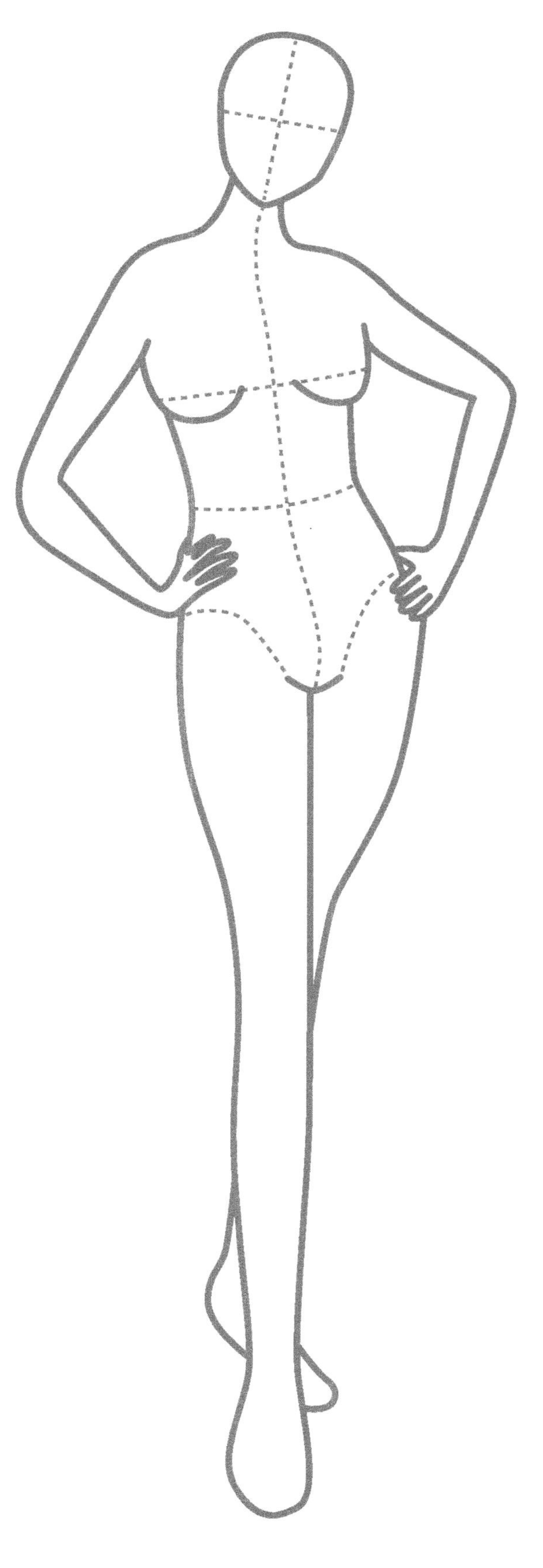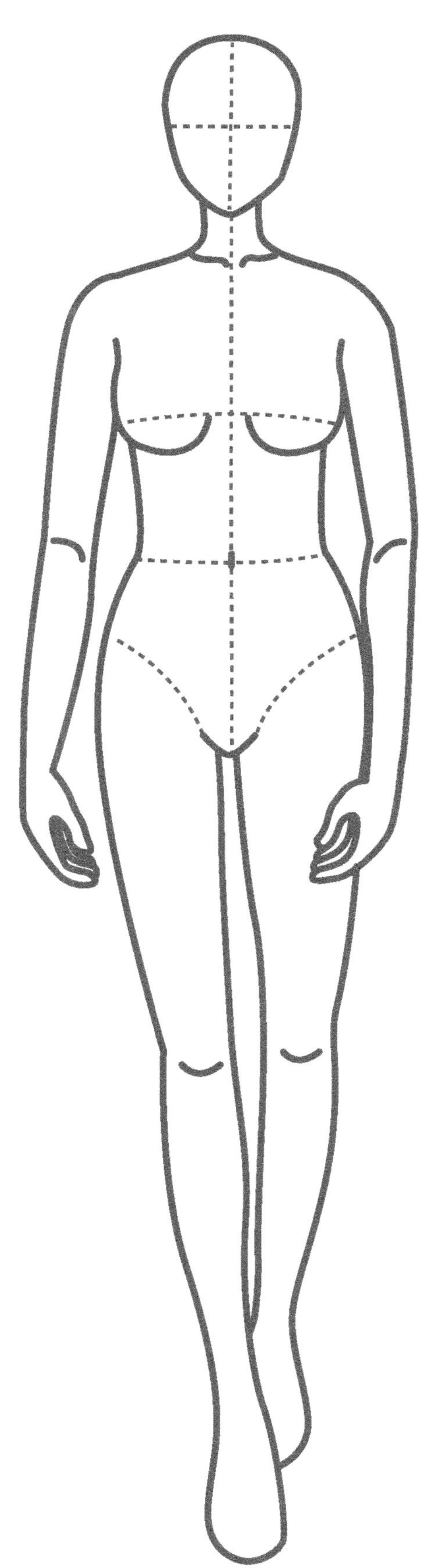

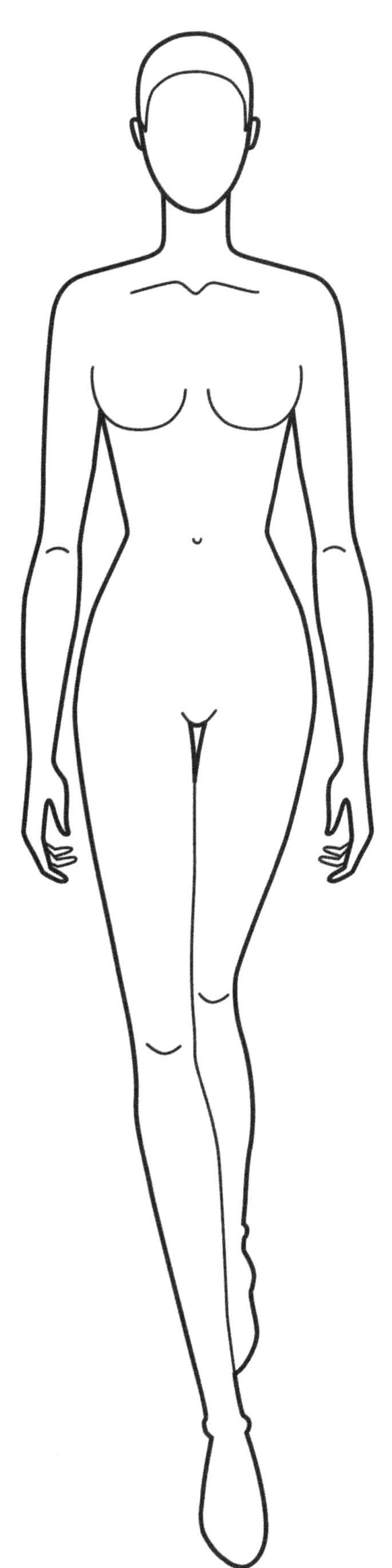
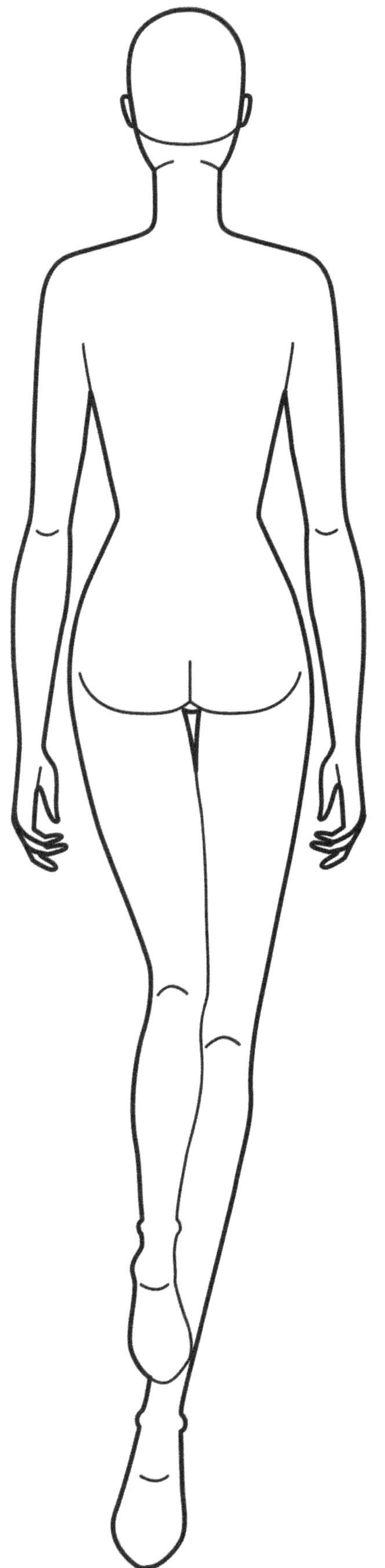

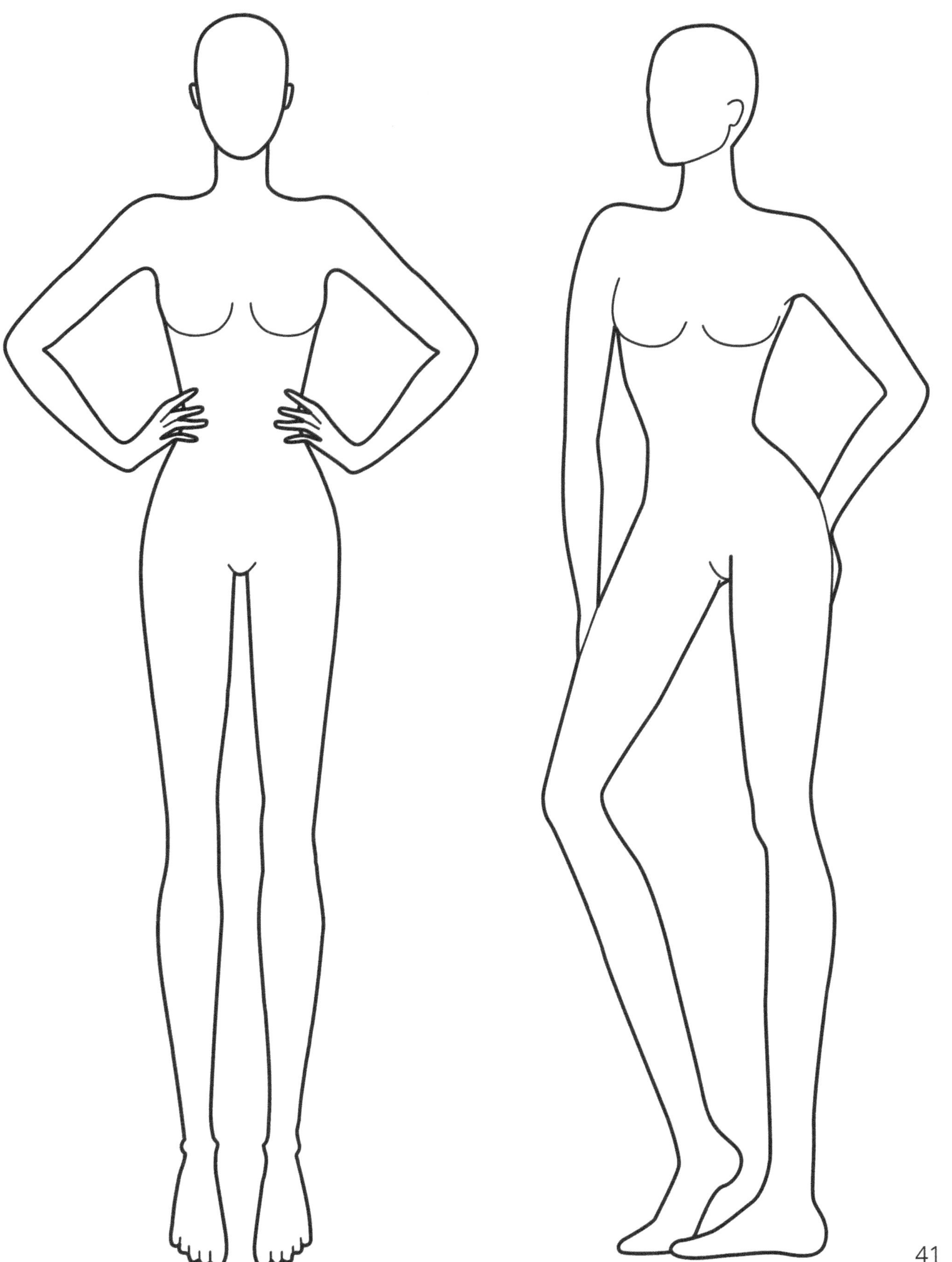

Your Notes & Inspiration Photos

This page is your creative gallery. Use it to track your progress, capture your favorite designs, and reflect on your journey.

- Add sketches, inspiration photos, or cutouts to bring your fashion ideas to life!
- Write down details such as colors, fabrics, or outfit elements that inspired you.
- Leave space for your future self to revisit and compare how your style evolves.

Pro Tip: *A single image or swatch can spark a whole collection. Don't be afraid to save even the smallest details that inspire you!*

Outfit Inspiration:
Office Chic and Runway Glam

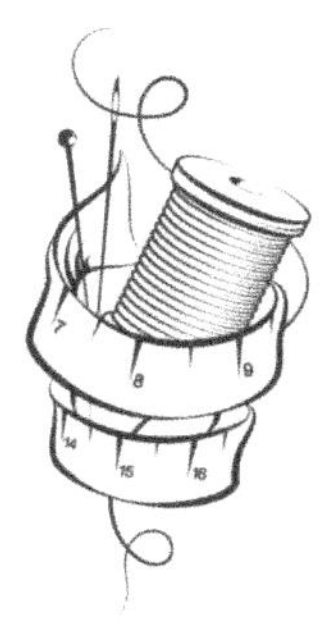

Classic Office Elegance and Red Carpet Glam

Office Chic Inspiration

A pencil skirt paired with a crisp blouse never goes out of style. Add a tailored blazer and mid-heel pumps for a polished silhouette that communicates confidence. Keep accessories minimal – a slim leather bag and a delicate watch create a refined balance. Neutral tones like navy, black, or cream ensure versatility, while a pop of red lipstick can instantly lift the look.

Runway Glam Inspiration

For a dramatic red carpet moment, think floor-length gowns with flowing fabrics. Silky satins and shimmering sequins create visual impact under bright lights. Experiment with daring necklines or open backs, and consider high slits for movement. Statement earrings or a bold clutch complete the glamorous aesthetic, ensuring the outfit feels stage-worthy yet balanced.

Fashion Practice Guide & Notes

Great design often comes from quick experiments. Don't overthink-let your hand move and capture the first idea that comes to mind. Spontaneity often reveals hidden creativity.

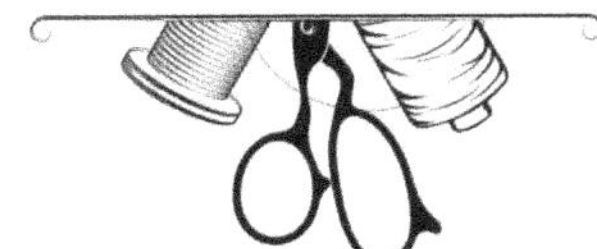

How to Use This Page:
- Create a 5-minute sketch to warm up.
- Focus on one element: sleeves, pants, or neckline.
- Annotate fabrics, textures, or color choices.

Reflection & Notes:
- Was I able to sketch faster than usual?
- What detail feels most successful in this design?
- What could I simplify next time?

Pro Tip*: Speed sketching builds confidence and sharpens your instincts.*

____

____

____

____

____

____

____

____

____

Outfit Inspiration: Streetwear

Athleisure Vibes: From the Gym to the Street

Athleisure blends comfort with edge. Think yoga leggings paired with oversized hoodies, cropped sweatshirts, or bomber jackets. The key is balance – tight on the bottom, relaxed on top, or the reverse.

Accessories make the look pop: baseball caps, chunky sneakers, crossbody fanny packs. Jewelry stays minimal to keep the sporty feel.

Fabric focus: breathable cotton, spandex, neoprene. Add one glossy or metallic piece to elevate the sporty vibe.

Pro Tip*: Athleisure is about confidence. Draw an outfit that looks ready for both a gym session and a café hangout.*

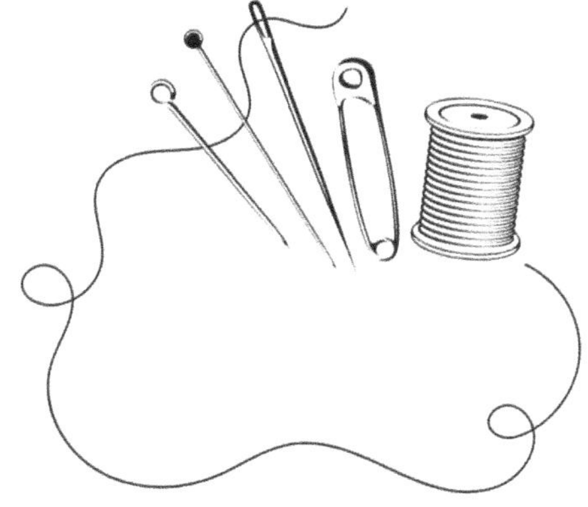

Trends

Inspiration

Textiles

Notes

Details

Swatches

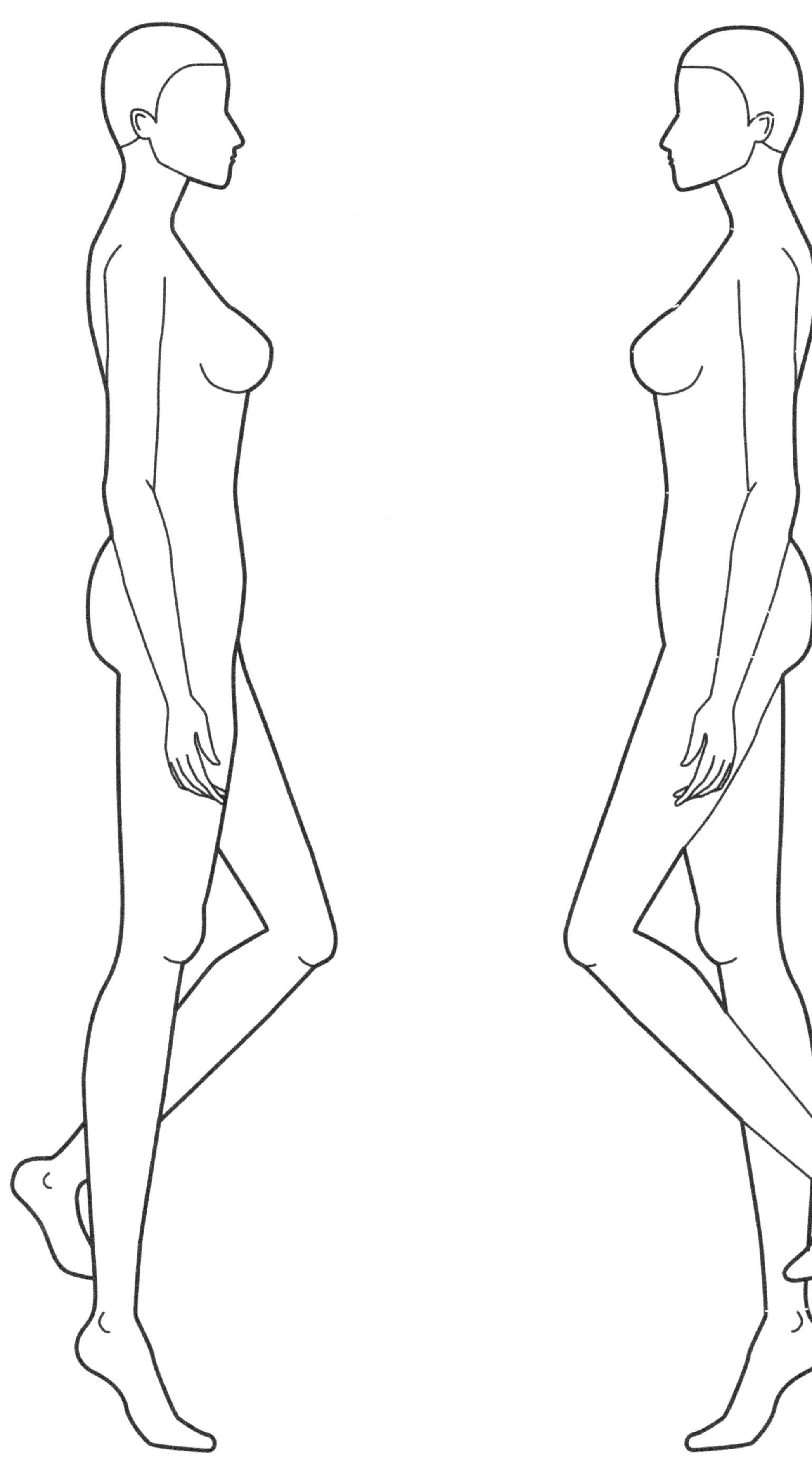

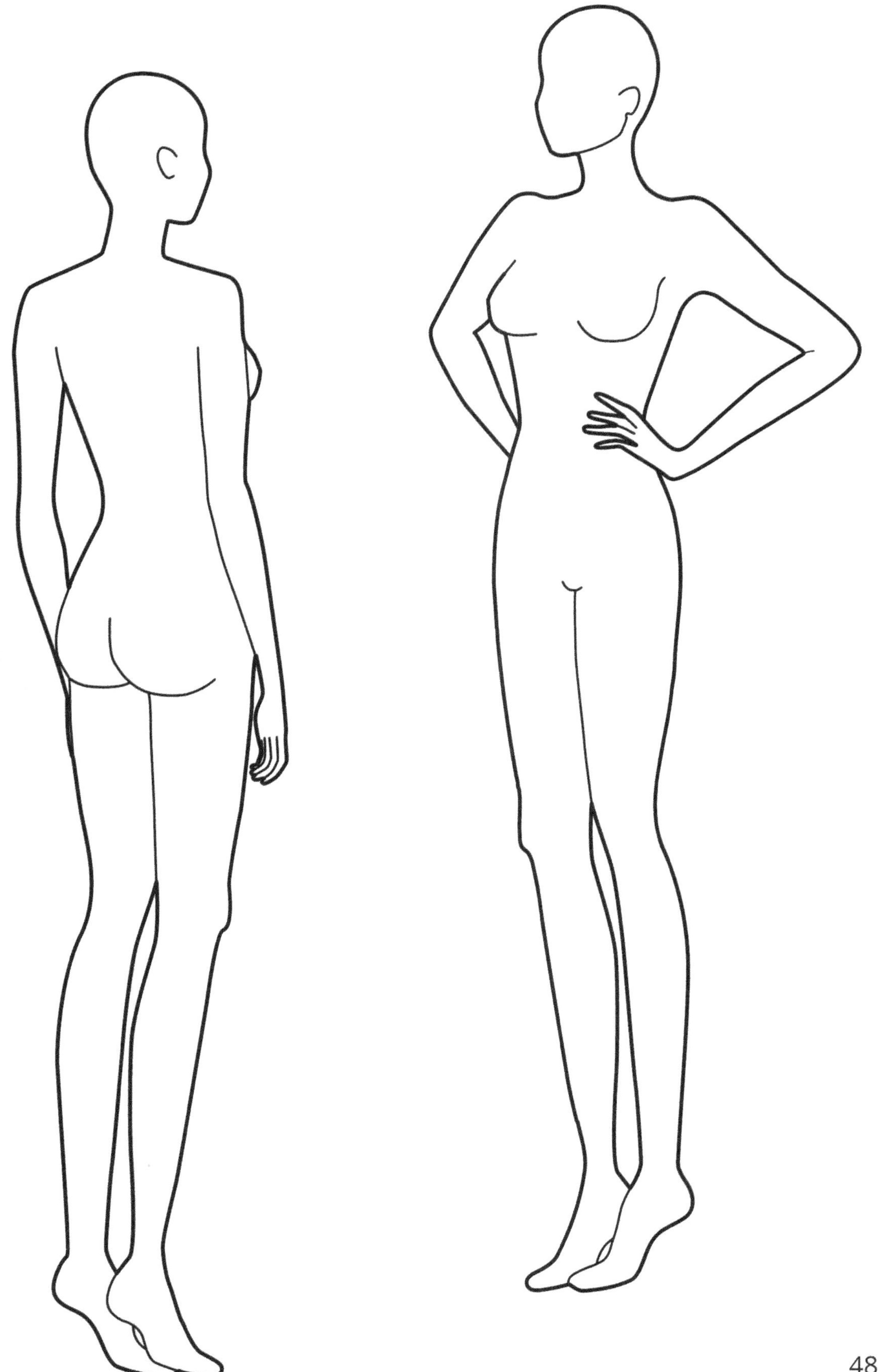

Your Notes & Inspiration Photos

This page is your creative gallery. Use it to track your progress, capture your favorite designs, and reflect on your journey.

- Add sketches, inspiration photos, or cutouts to bring your fashion ideas to life!
- Write down details such as colors, fabrics, or outfit elements that inspired you.
- Leave space for your future self to revisit and compare how your style evolves.

Pro Tip: *A single image or swatch can spark a whole collection. Don't be afraid to save even the smallest details that inspire you!*

Outfit Inspiration:
Office Chic and Runway Glam

Minimalist Professional and Futuristic Runway

Office Chic Inspiration

Minimalism thrives in the office environment. Pair straight-cut trousers with a monochrome top and a longline blazer. Opt for sleek fabrics that drape well, and keep the palette in black, white, or beige for a modern edge. Shoes should be equally simple – loafers or pointed flats are both chic and practical. The power of this style is in clean lines and quiet confidence.

Runway Glam Inspiration

Futuristic fashion brings bold experimentation. Picture metallic fabrics, asymmetrical cuts, and exaggerated shoulders. Geometric shapes in silver or iridescent tones can push boundaries while staying wearable. Pair these dramatic silhouettes with minimal accessories to let the structure speak for itself. Futuristic glam is about confidence and vision – perfect for the spotlight.

Fashion Practice Guide & Notes

Clothing tells a story. Let this page be your stage to design an outfit inspired by a theme, emotion, or even a place. The more personal the inspiration, the stronger the design.

How to Use This Page:
- Choose a concept (travel, nightlife, minimalism).
- Translate it into shapes, lines, and accessories.
- Add details that connect the outfit to the story.

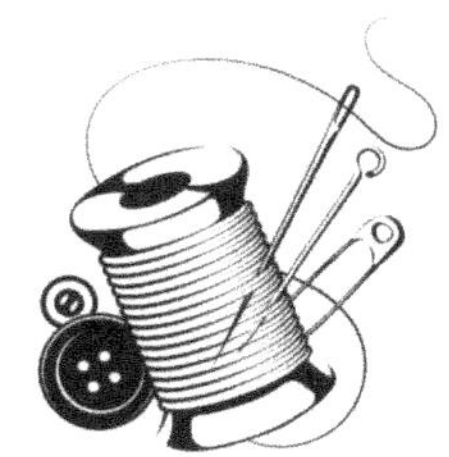

Reflection & Notes:
- Did my sketch capture the theme I chose?
- Which element best communicates the story?
- How could I push this concept further?

Pro Tip: *A strong design always carries meaning beyond the fabric.*

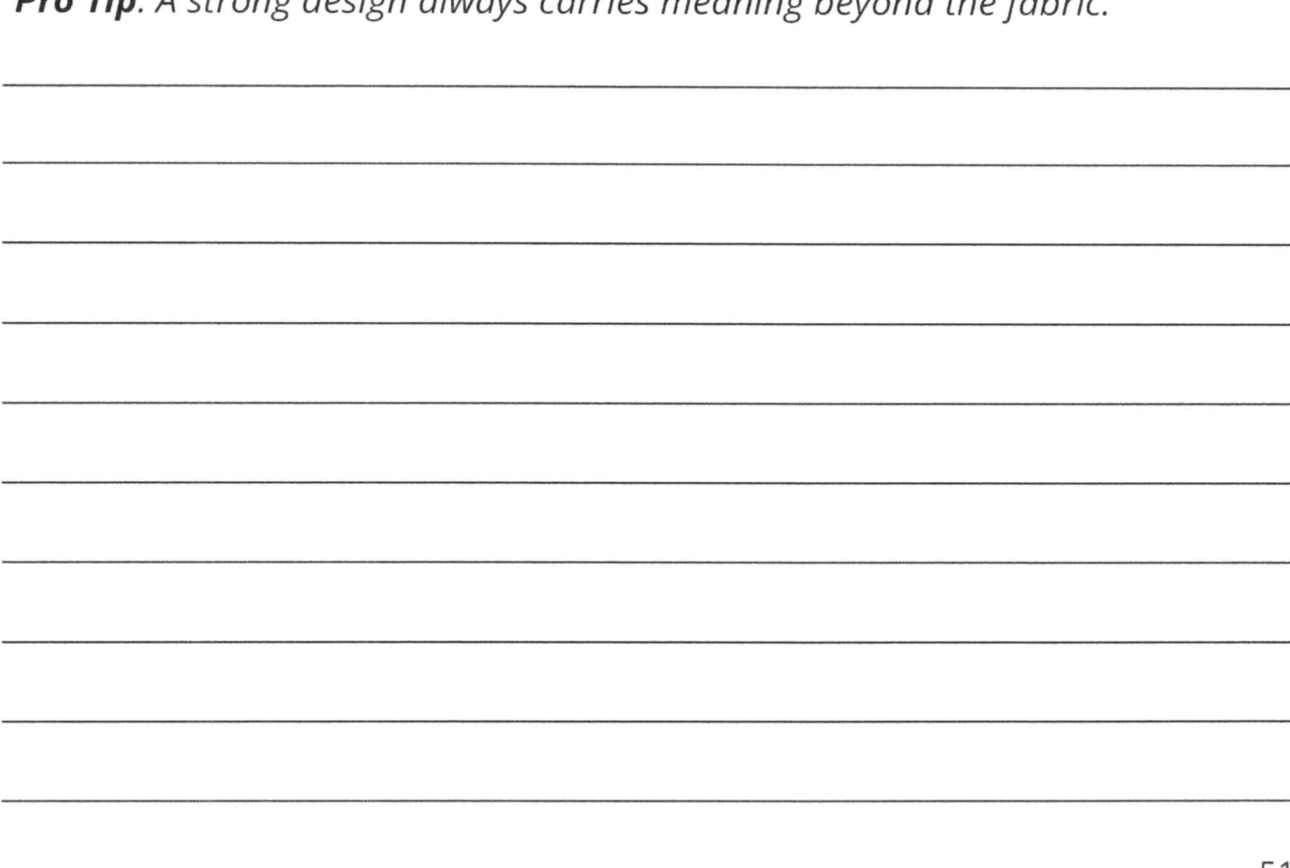

Outfit Inspiration: Streetwear

Denim Culture: The Core of Urban Style

Denim is the backbone of streetwear. High-waisted jeans, cropped jackets, patchwork skirts, or distressed shorts – all carry the urban edge. Wide-leg cuts scream retro, while ripped skinny jeans add rebellion.

Double-denim is trending again. Sketch a dark denim bottom with a lighter oversized jacket to create contrast. Add sneakers or boots to complete the street mood.

Customization counts: embroidery, graffiti-inspired prints, or intentional frays make denim designs unique.

Try this: imagine a denim jumpsuit styled with sneakers and bold sunglasses – functional, stylish, and street-ready.

Trends

Inspiration

Textiles

Notes

Details

Swatches

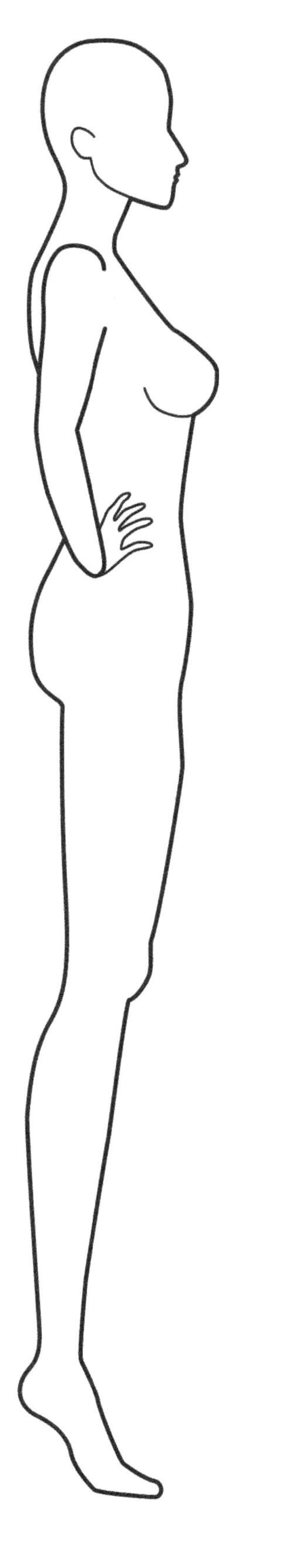
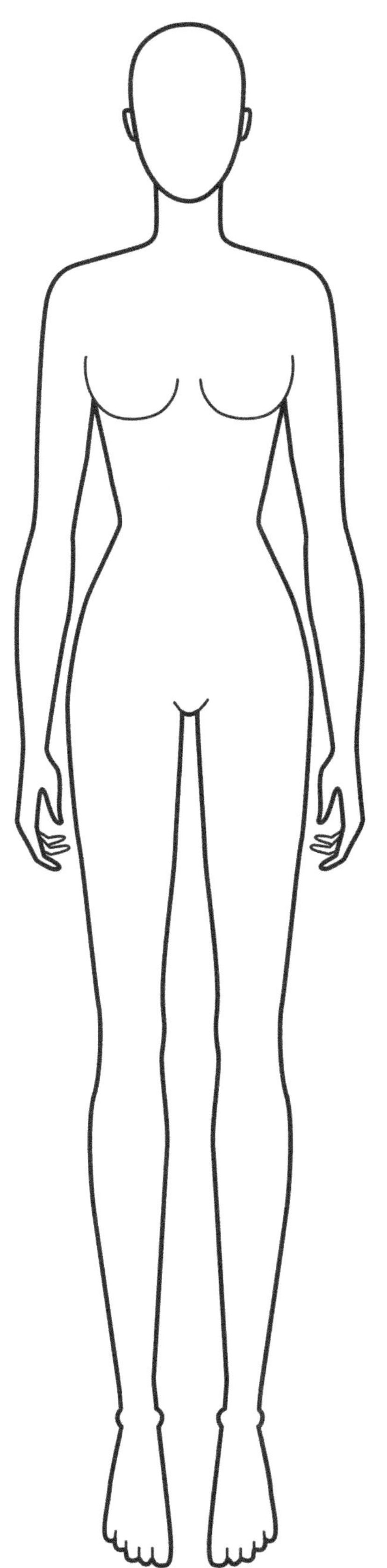

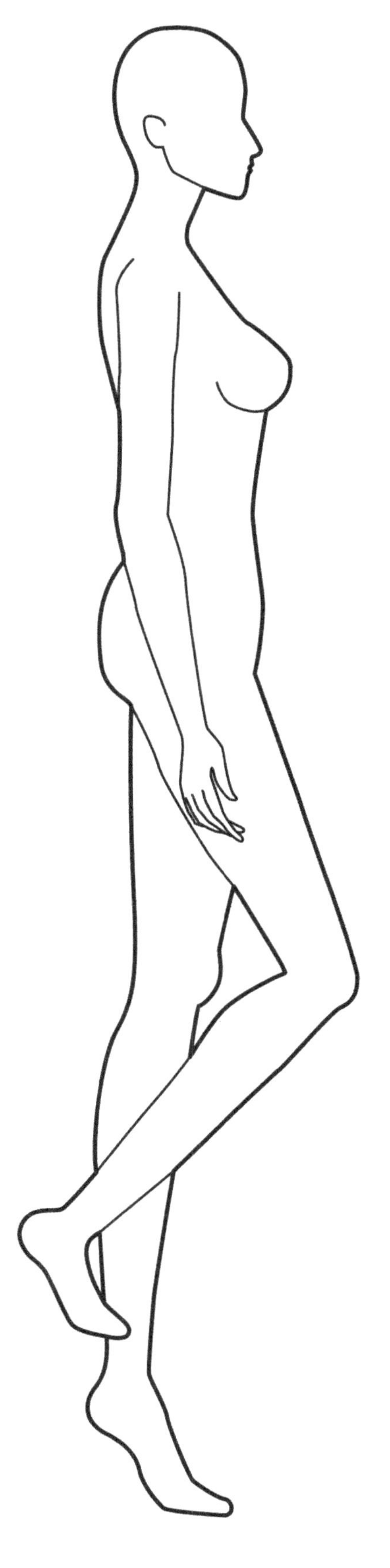
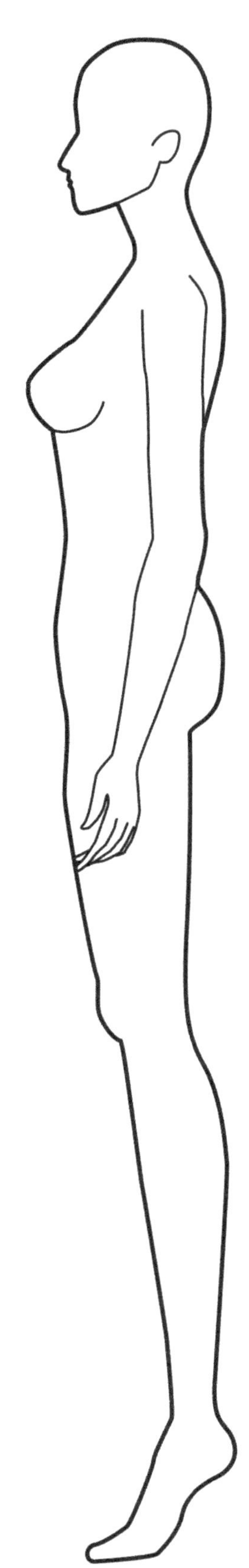

Your Notes & Inspiration Photos

This page is your creative gallery. Use it to track your progress, capture your favorite designs, and reflect on your journey.

- Add sketches, inspiration photos, or cutouts to bring your fashion ideas to life!
- Write down details such as colors, fabrics, or outfit elements that inspired you.
- Leave space for your future self to revisit and compare how your style evolves.

Pro Tip: *A single image or swatch can spark a whole collection. Don't be afraid to save even the smallest details that inspire you!*

Outfit Inspiration:
Office Chic and Runway Glam

Creative Professional and Festival Glam

Office Chic Inspiration

For women working in creative industries, the office outfit can be both polished and expressive. Wide-leg trousers in bold colors, paired with patterned blouses or statement jewelry, strike the right balance. Layer with a light trench coat or oversized cardigan for depth. The goal is to project professionalism without hiding creativity.

Runway Glam Inspiration

Festival-inspired glam brings vibrancy and energy. Think flowing maxi dresses, fringe details, and colorful embroidery. Shimmery fabrics like lamé or metallic mesh catch light beautifully during movement. Add bold accessories – oversized earrings, chunky bracelets, or embellished belts – to amplify the festive spirit.

Fashion Practice Guide & Notes

 Think of this page as your fashion lab. Test ideas, combine elements that don't usually go together, and see what happens. Innovation often comes from breaking rules.

How to Use This Page:
- Mix two contrasting styles (casual vs. formal, minimal vs. oversized).
- Add accessories that shift the outfit's mood.
- Write notes about what worked and what clashed.

Reflection & Notes:

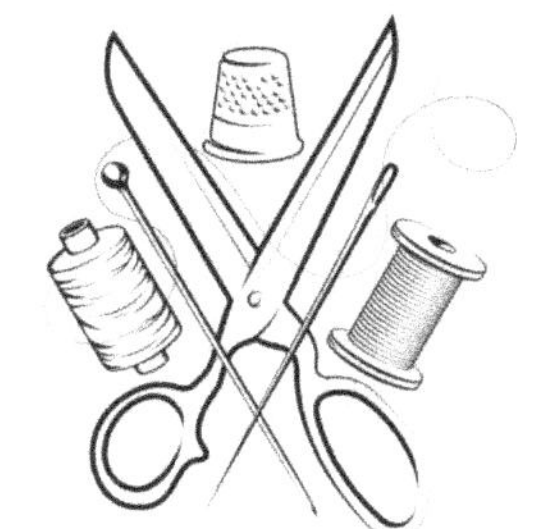

- Did I discover a new combination today?
- What surprised me most about this design?
- Would this outfit work in real life?

Pro Tip: *Unusual pairings can create unforgettable looks.*

____

____

____

____

____

____

____

____

____

Outfit Inspiration: Streetwear

Oversized Energy: Playing with Volume

Oversized pieces give streetwear its bold identity. Picture an extra-large hoodie that falls mid-thigh, or cargo pants with exaggerated wide legs.

Balance is essential. Combine oversized tops with slim bottoms, or vice versa. Crop tops also pair perfectly with baggy jeans or joggers.

Color direction: neutrals dominate, but one bold neon or pastel piece becomes the focal point.

Pro Tip: *In your sketch, exaggerate volume slightly – longer sleeves, larger hoods, or baggier trousers – to capture the oversized aesthetic.*

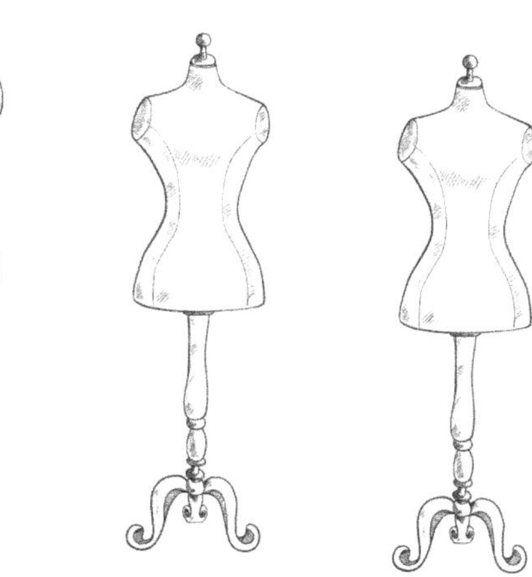

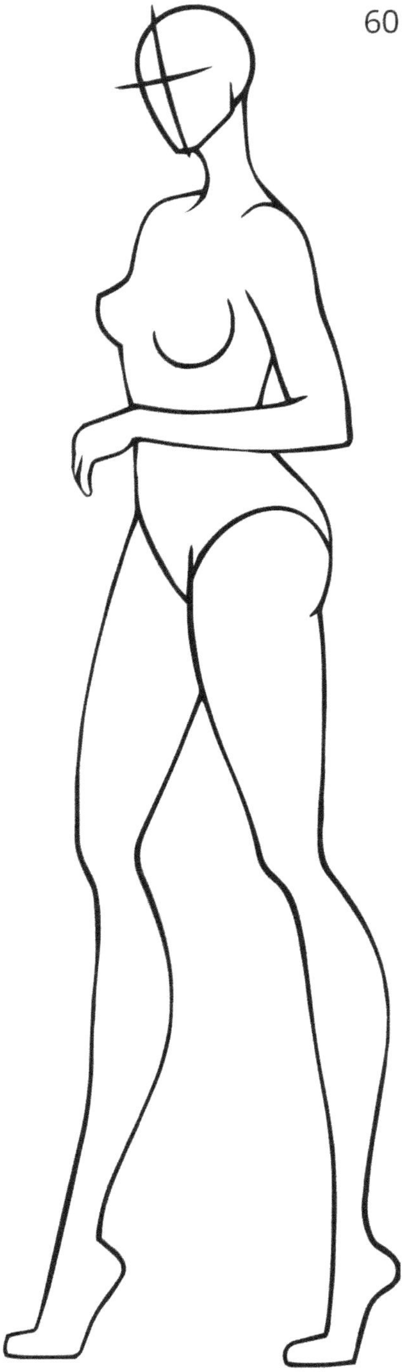

Trends

Inspiration

Textiles

Notes

Details

Swatches

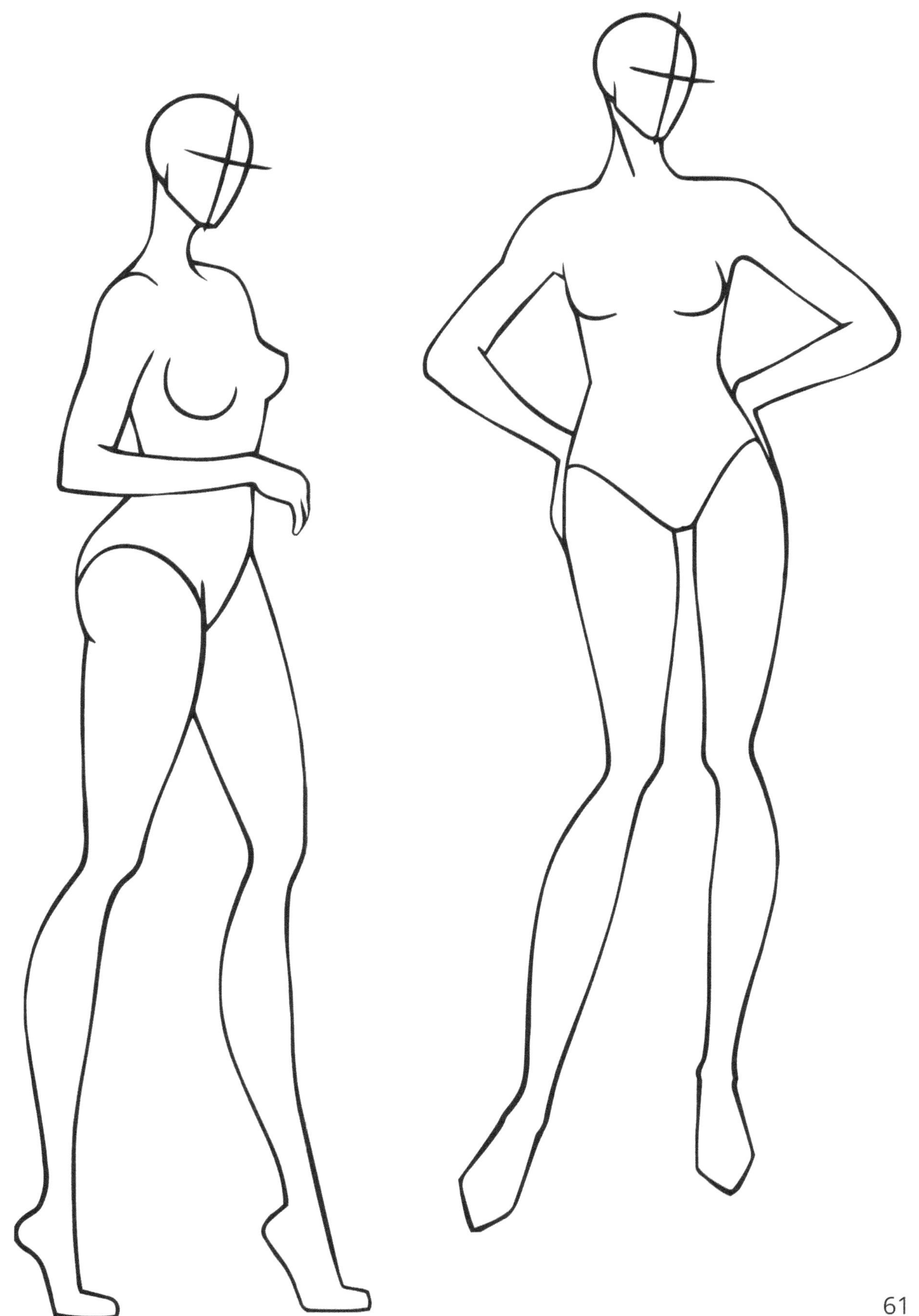

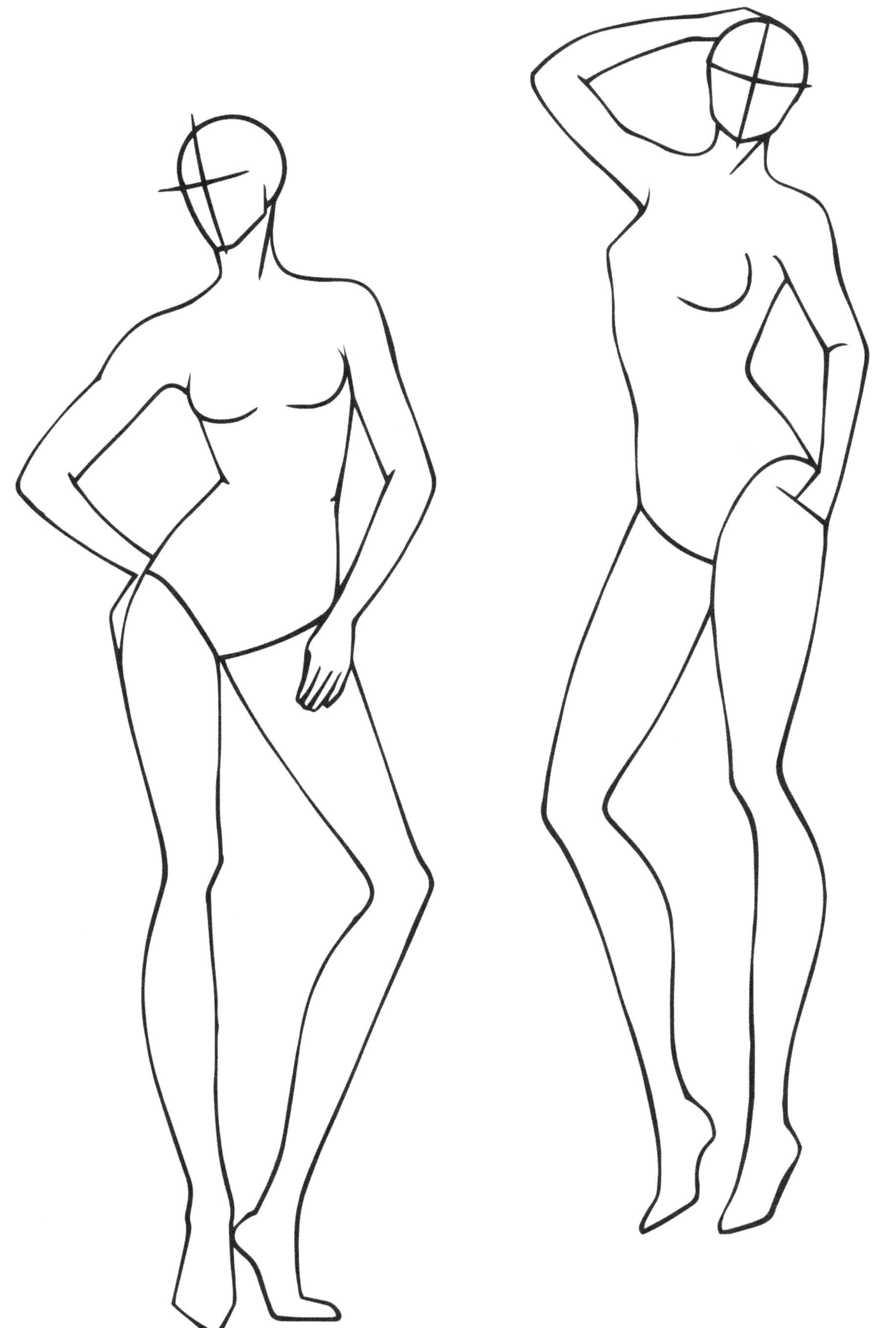

Your Notes & Inspiration Photos

This page is your creative gallery. Use it to track your progress, capture your favorite designs, and reflect on your journey.

- Add sketches, inspiration photos, or cutouts to bring your fashion ideas to life!
- Write down details such as colors, fabrics, or outfit elements that inspired you.
- Leave space for your future self to revisit and compare how your style evolves.

Pro Tip: *A single image or swatch can spark a whole collection. Don't be afraid to save even the smallest details that inspire you!*

Outfit Inspiration:
Office Chic and Runway Glam

Power Dressing and Sustainable Glam

Office Chic Inspiration

Power dressing emphasizes sharp tailoring. A double-breasted blazer, wide-shouldered silhouette, and structured handbag communicate authority. Pair with slim-fit trousers or a fitted dress to balance volume. Strong colors like deep burgundy or forest green add impact while keeping sophistication intact.

Runway Glam Inspiration

Sustainable glam is about making bold fashion statements responsibly. Experiment with organic fabrics, recycled textiles, and natural dyes. Create runway looks that prove eco-conscious choices can be just as dazzling. Flowy gowns in earthy tones, accented with upcycled jewelry, highlight the beauty of ethical fashion.

Fashion Practice Guide & Notes

Fashion is also about function. Use this page to think practically: is the outfit wearable, comfortable, and versatile? Sketching with purpose makes designs stronger.

How to Use This Page:
- Design for a specific occasion (work, travel, leisure).
- Consider movement: can someone walk, sit, or dance in it?
- Add notes about practicality (fabric, fit, comfort).

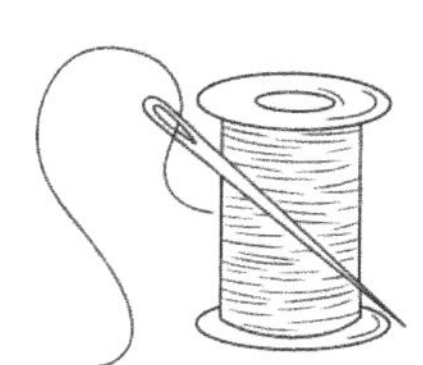

Reflection & Notes:
- Did I balance style with comfort?
- Which detail makes the outfit most wearable?
- How could I adapt this design for another occasion?

Pro Tip: *Practical details often elevate a design from concept to reality.*

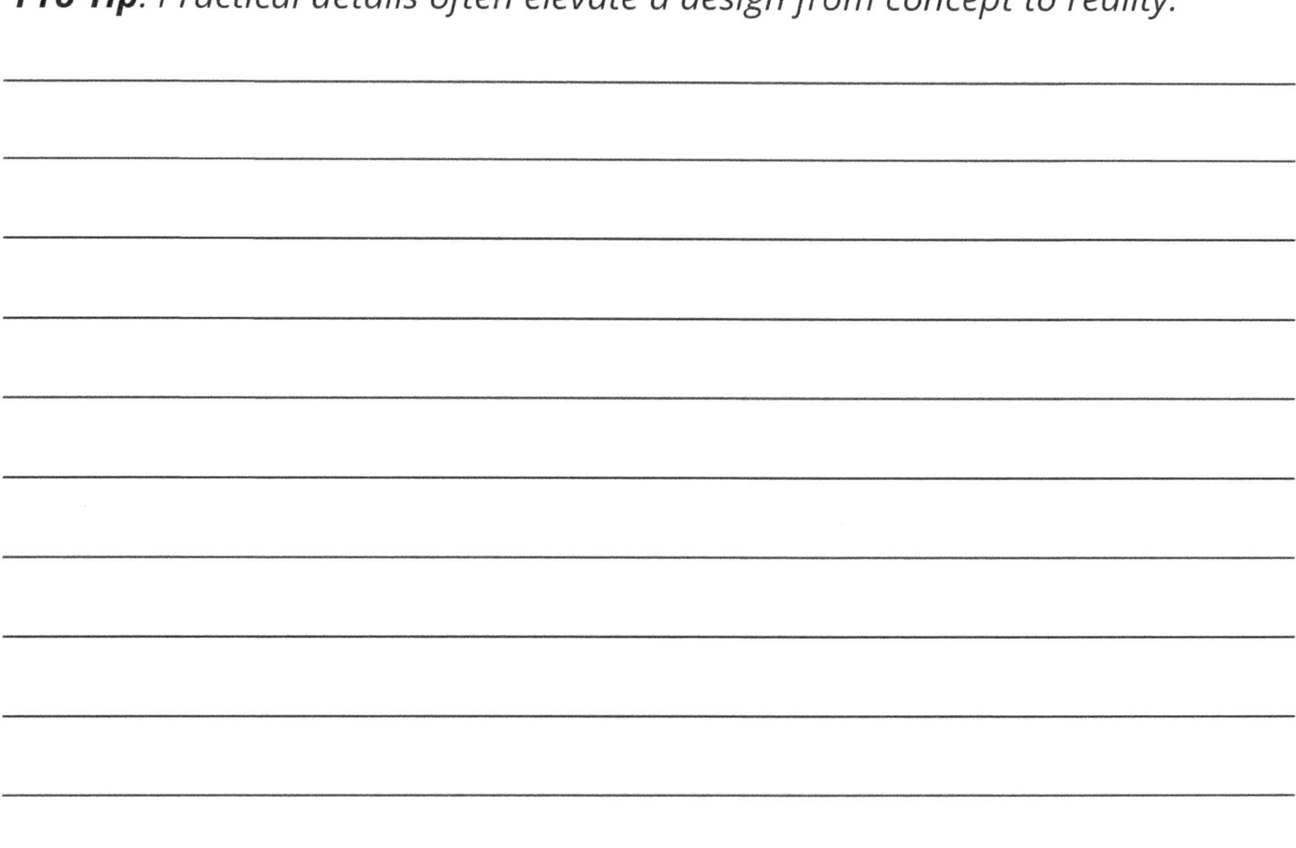

Outfit Inspiration: Streetwear

Graphic Statements

Streetwear is often loud, unapologetic, and expressive. Graphic prints and slogans are a key way to communicate attitude. Oversized tees with bold text, hoodies with cartoon-style illustrations, or jackets with back prints – they're all wearable art.

Design exercise: sketch a plain hoodie, then fill the back with a graphic. It could be abstract art, a nature motif, or a bold word that reflects empowerment.

Fabric tip: screen-printing, embroidery, or patchwork can be used in real life – but on paper, your creativity has no limits.

Trends

Inspiration

Textiles

Notes

Details

Swatches

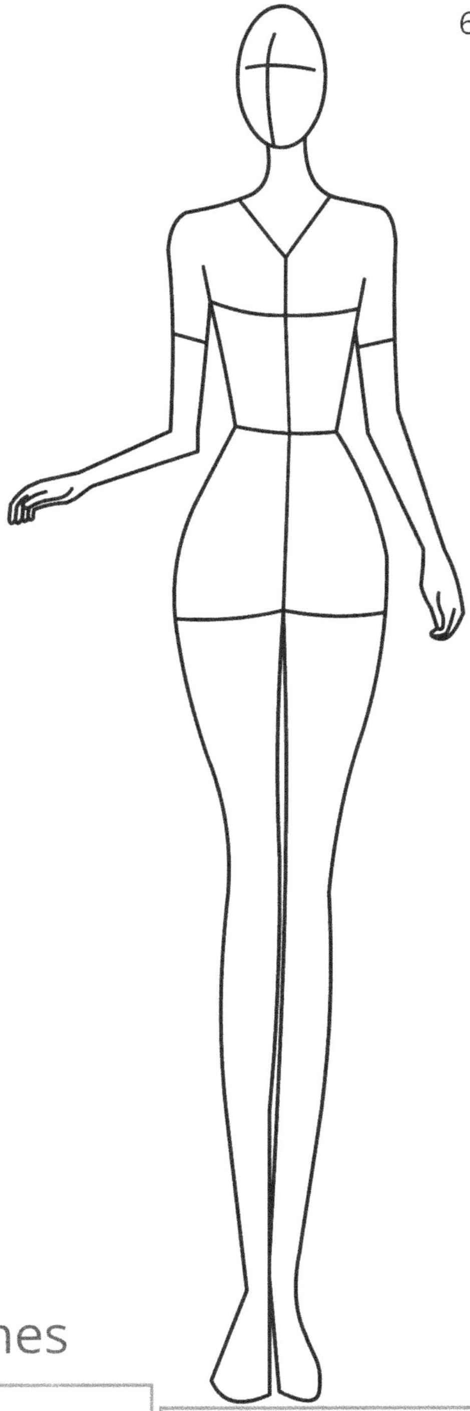

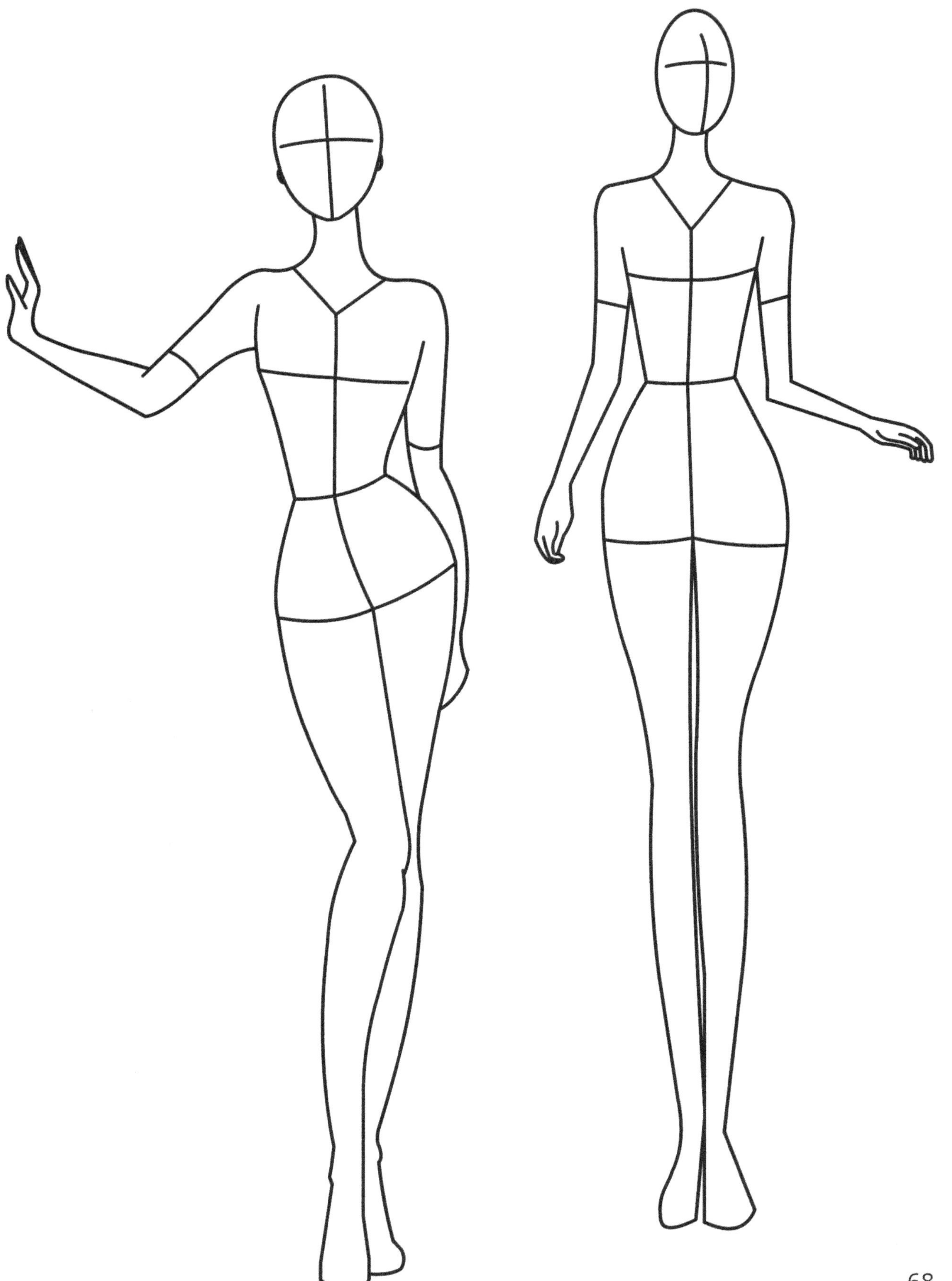

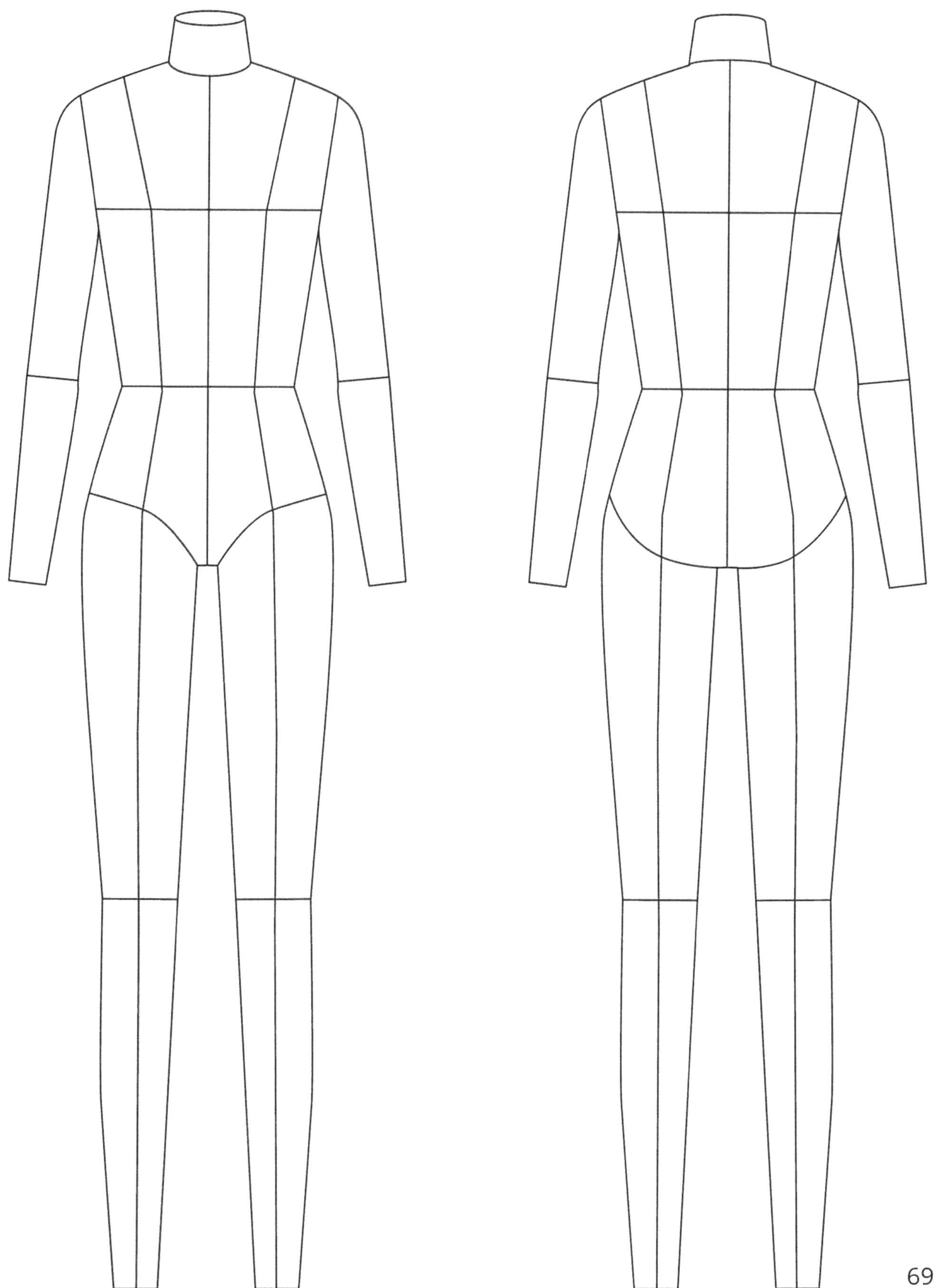

Your Notes & Inspiration Photos

This page is your creative gallery. Use it to track your progress, capture your favorite designs, and reflect on your journey.

- Add sketches, inspiration photos, or cutouts to bring your fashion ideas to life!
- Write down details such as colors, fabrics, or outfit elements that inspired you.
- Leave space for your future self to revisit and compare how your style evolves.

Pro Tip: *A single image or swatch can spark a whole collection. Don't be afraid to save even the smallest details that inspire you!*

Outfit Inspiration:
Office Chic and Runway Glam

Relaxed Friday Look and Haute Couture Glam

Office Chic Inspiration

Casual Fridays open the door to more relaxed combinations. Dark denim paired with a silk blouse and a smart blazer bridges professionalism with comfort. Shoes can range from sleek ankle boots to clean white sneakers. Keep the look polished with structured accessories – a tote bag or slim belt ties it together.

Runway Glam Inspiration

Haute couture embodies artistry. Elaborate hand-sewn embellishments, luxurious fabrics, and avant-garde silhouettes transform garments into wearable sculptures. Consider exaggerated ruffles, dramatic trains, or intricate embroidery. These pieces push the limits of craftsmanship and make runway presentations unforgettable.

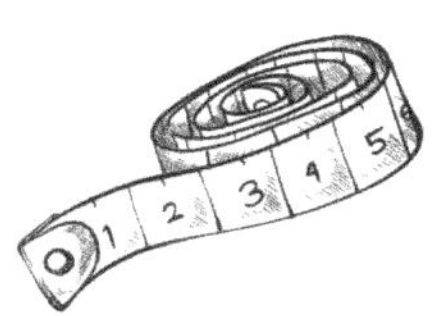

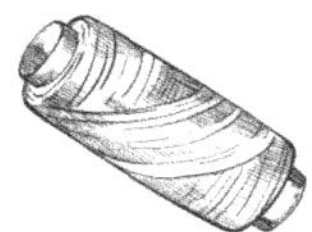

Fashion Practice Guide & Notes

Textures bring clothing to life. Use this page to imagine fabrics, surfaces, and materials. Even a flat sketch can feel tactile when details are clear.

How to Use This Page:
- Sketch garments and label fabrics (denim, silk, wool, mesh).
- Experiment with mixing light and heavy textures.
- Use notes to describe how the fabric should move.

Reflection & Notes:
- Which fabric combination works best here?
- Did I balance texture with silhouette?
- How would I improve the visual impact?

Pro Tip: Texture is the secret ingredient that makes outfits memorable.

Outfit Inspiration: Streetwear

Streetwear in Neutrals

Not all streetwear is flashy. Minimalist neutral tones (black, beige, grey, white) are a powerful direction. These outfits focus on clean shapes and simple layers.

Think beige joggers, black crop tops, oversized grey coats, and white sneakers. Accessories stay subtle: caps, small backpacks, minimal jewelry.

Sketch exercise: design a monochrome streetwear outfit, then add one contrasting element (for example, a red belt or neon shoes) to see how the accent shifts the entire vibe.

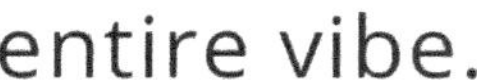

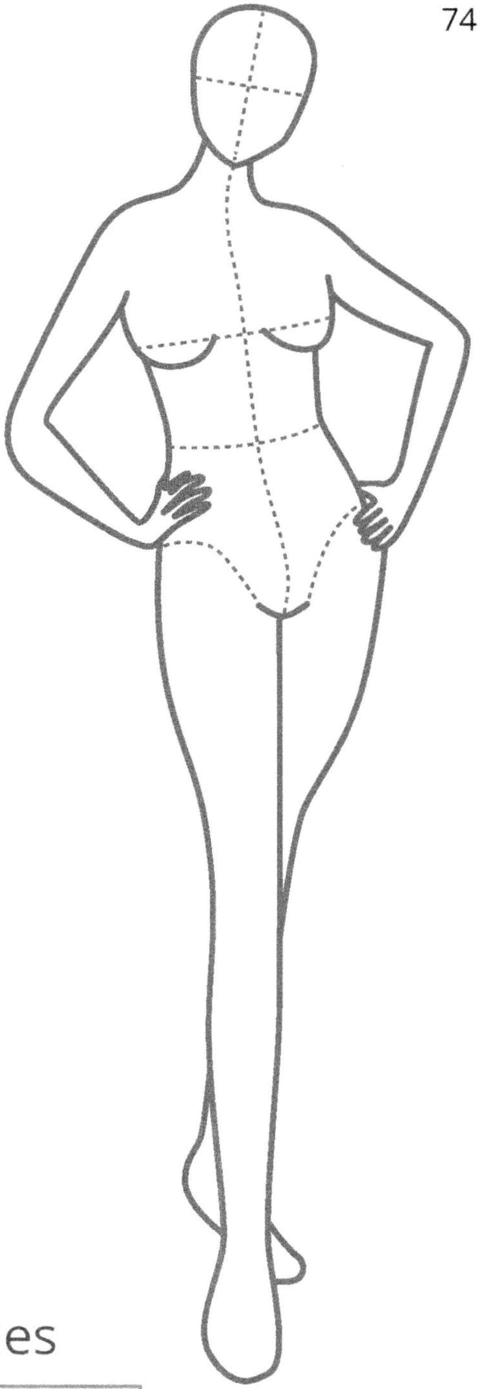

Trends

Inspiration

Textiles

Notes

Details

Swatches

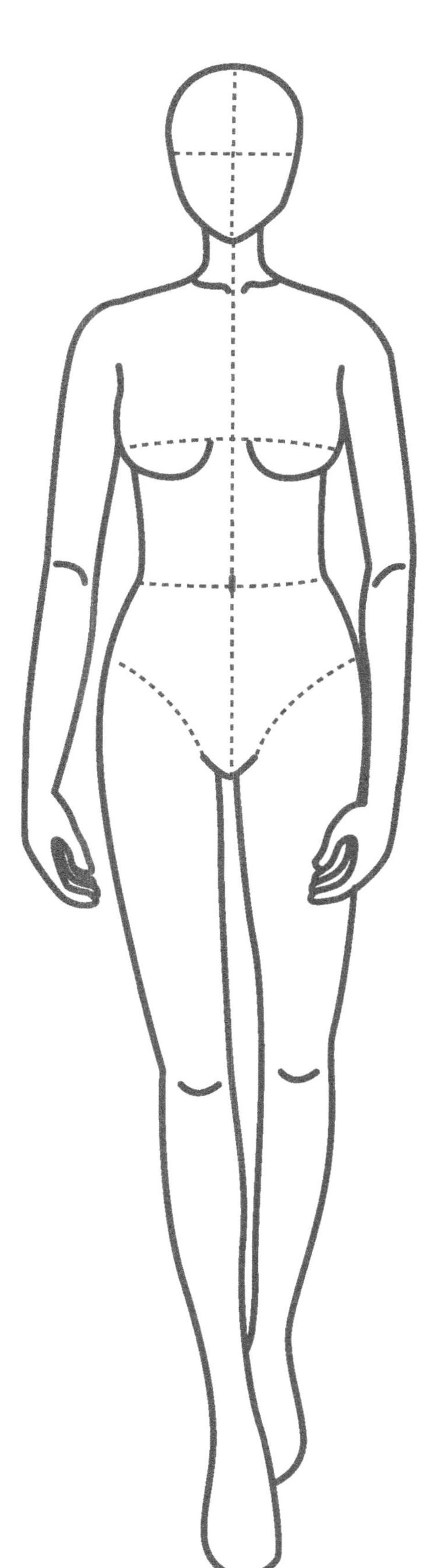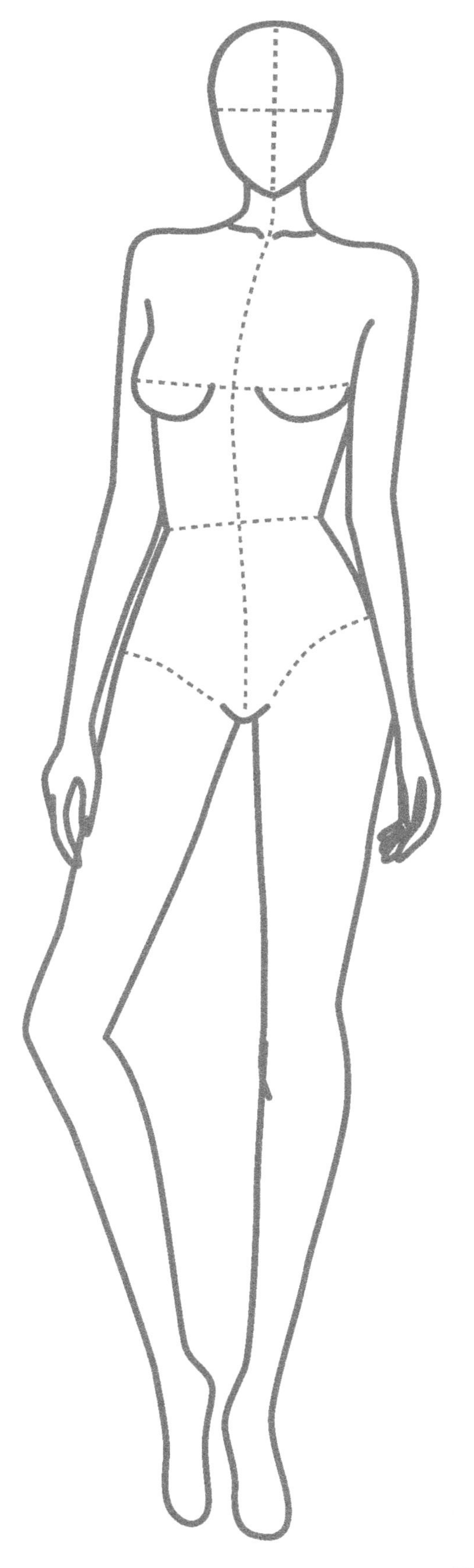

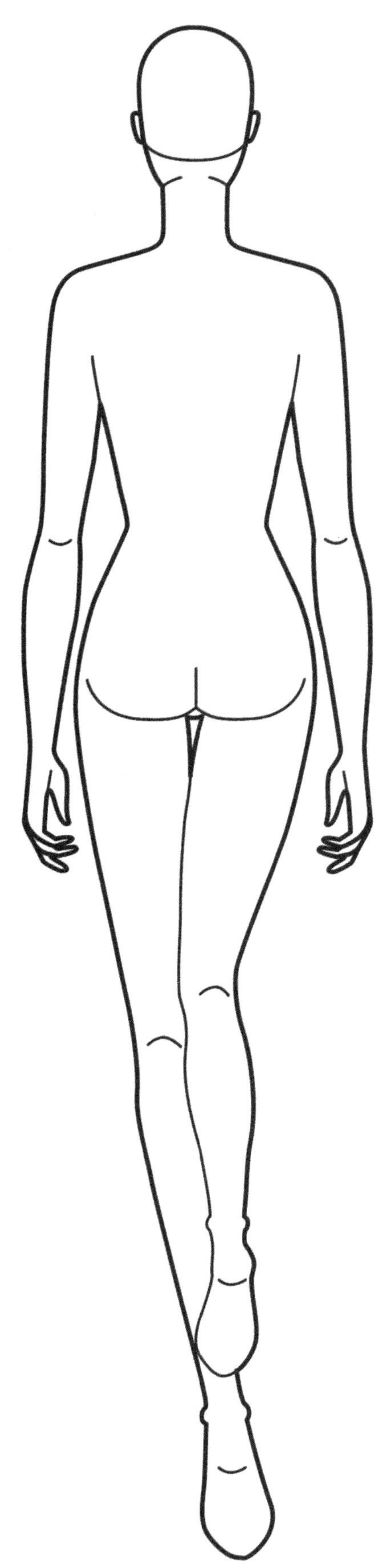
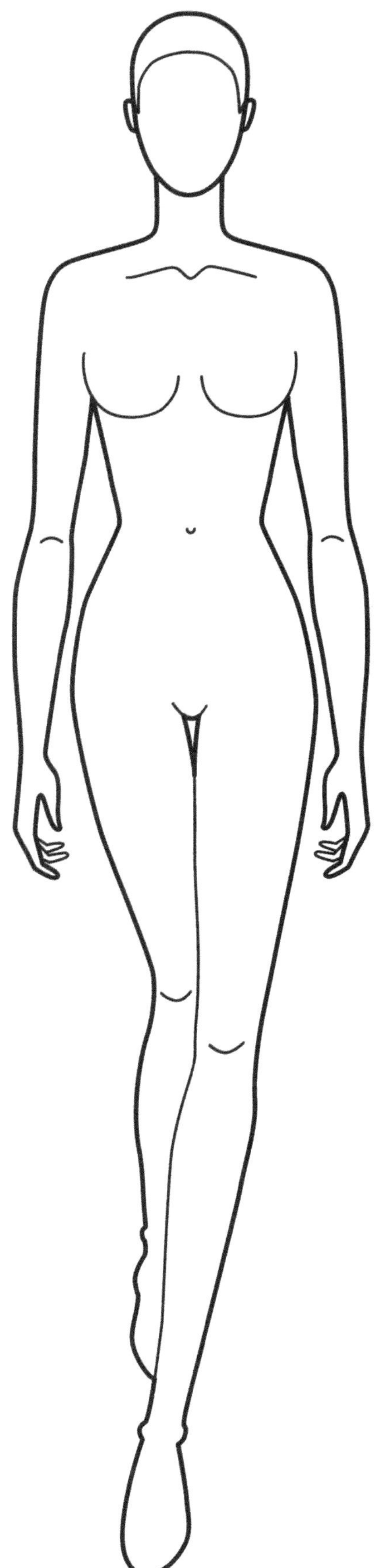

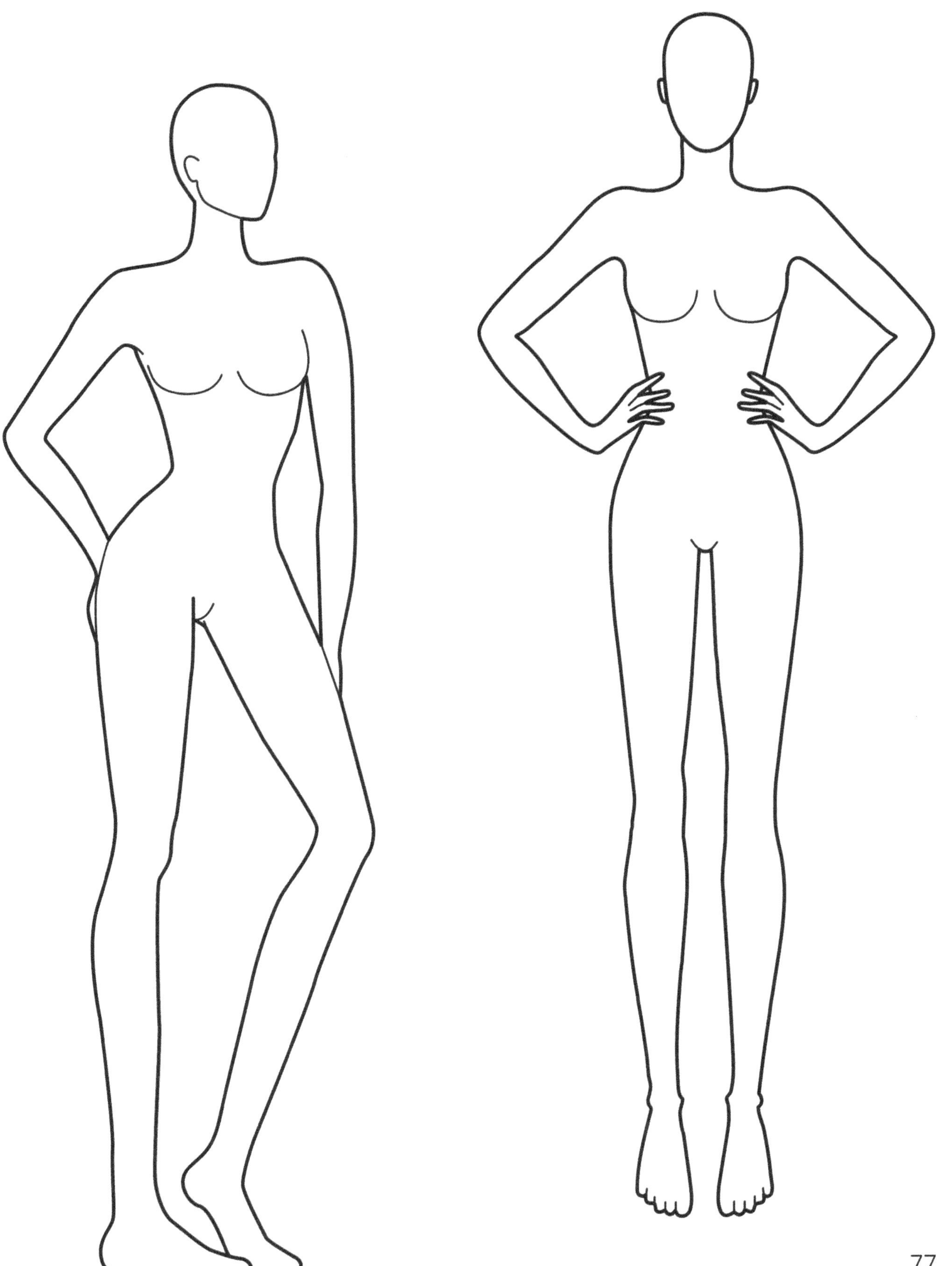

Your Notes & Inspiration Photos

This page is your creative gallery. Use it to track your progress, capture your favorite designs, and reflect on your journey.

- Add sketches, inspiration photos, or cutouts to bring your fashion ideas to life!
- Write down details such as colors, fabrics, or outfit elements that inspired you.
- Leave space for your future self to revisit and compare how your style evolves.

Pro Tip: *A single image or swatch can spark a whole collection. Don't be afraid to save even the smallest details that inspire you!*

Outfit Inspiration:
Office Chic and Runway Glam

Monochrome Office Style and Minimal Runway Glam

Office Chic Inspiration

A monochrome look instantly feels cohesive. Choose one color family – all beige, all grey, or all navy – and layer different textures within it. A wool skirt, silk blouse, and leather belt in matching tones elevate the ensemble while keeping it subtle. Minimal jewelry reinforces the sophistication of the look.

Runway Glam Inspiration

Minimal glam celebrates simplicity. Long dresses with sleek lines, no excess embellishment, and solid, bold colors like emerald or cobalt create a striking effect. Pair with a single standout accessory, such as chandelier earrings or a sculptural clutch. Less is more, but the impact is unforgettable.

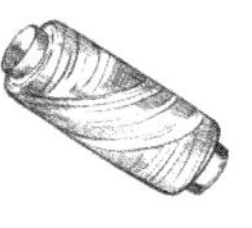
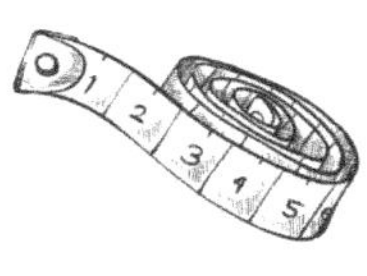

Fashion Practice Guide & Notes

Accessories can transform an outfit completely. Use this page to test how bags, shoes, or jewelry elevate your sketch.

How to Use This Page:
- Start with a simple base outfit.
- Add 2–3 different accessory sets.
- Write which version feels strongest.

Reflection & Notes:
- Which accessory added the most character?
- Did the accessories overpower or enhance the outfit?
- How could I refine balance between outfit and add-ons?

Pro Tip: *Accessories are small details that create big statements.*

Outfit Inspiration: Streetwear

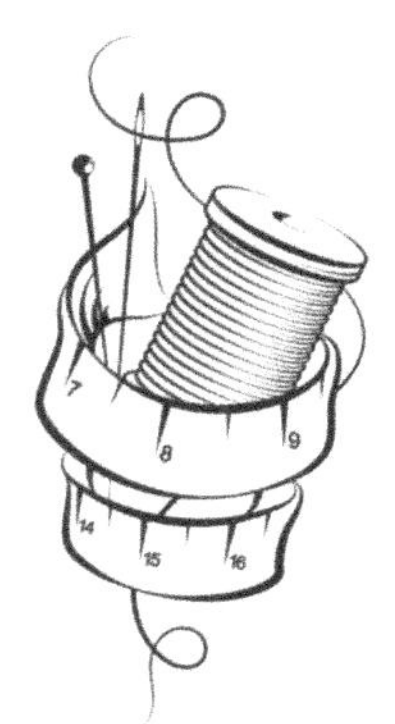

Streetwear with Feminine Touches

Streetwear doesn't have to mean "tomboy." Adding feminine details creates balance: skirts paired with sneakers, slip dresses layered over tees, or oversized hoodies worn with thigh-high socks.

Fabric inspiration: satin skirts with bomber jackets, lace tops with denim shorts. Mixing hard and soft textures creates a fresh, unique look.

Sketch challenge: design an outfit that includes both a feminine element (like a skirt) and a classic streetwear staple (like sneakers or a hoodie).

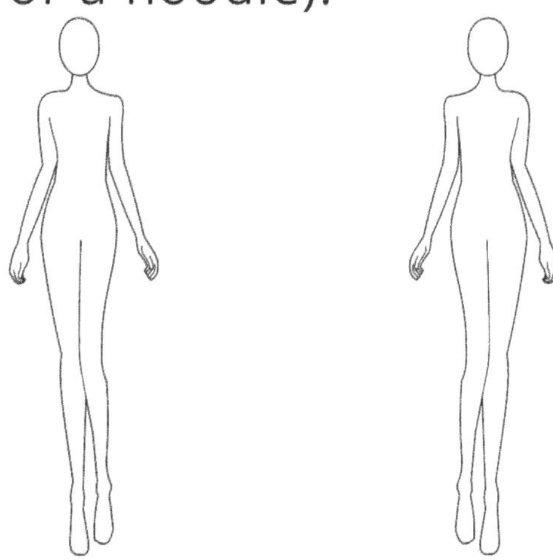

Trends

Inspiration

Textiles

Notes

Details

Swatches

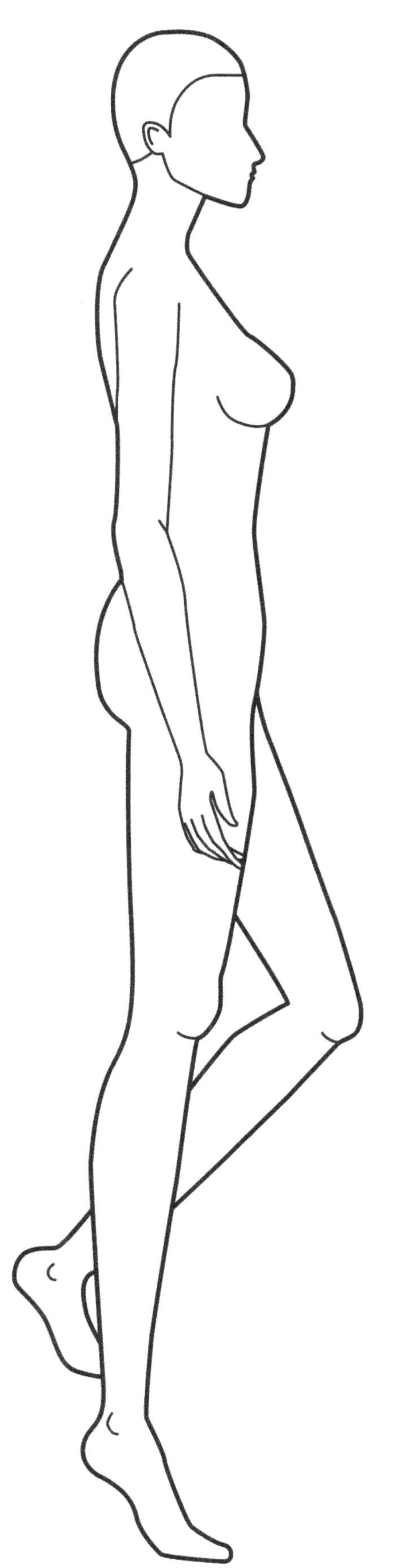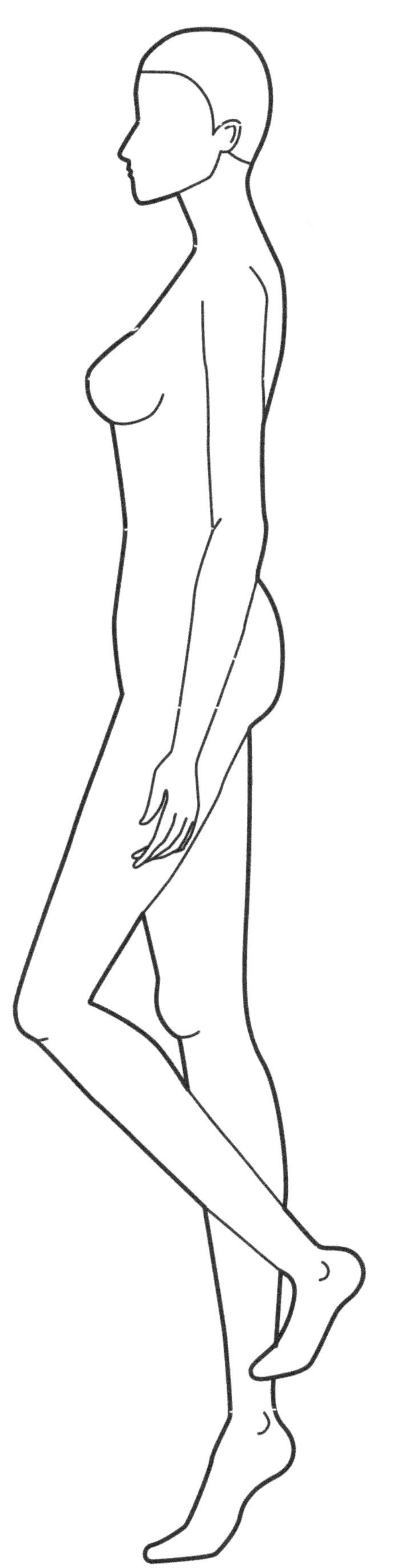

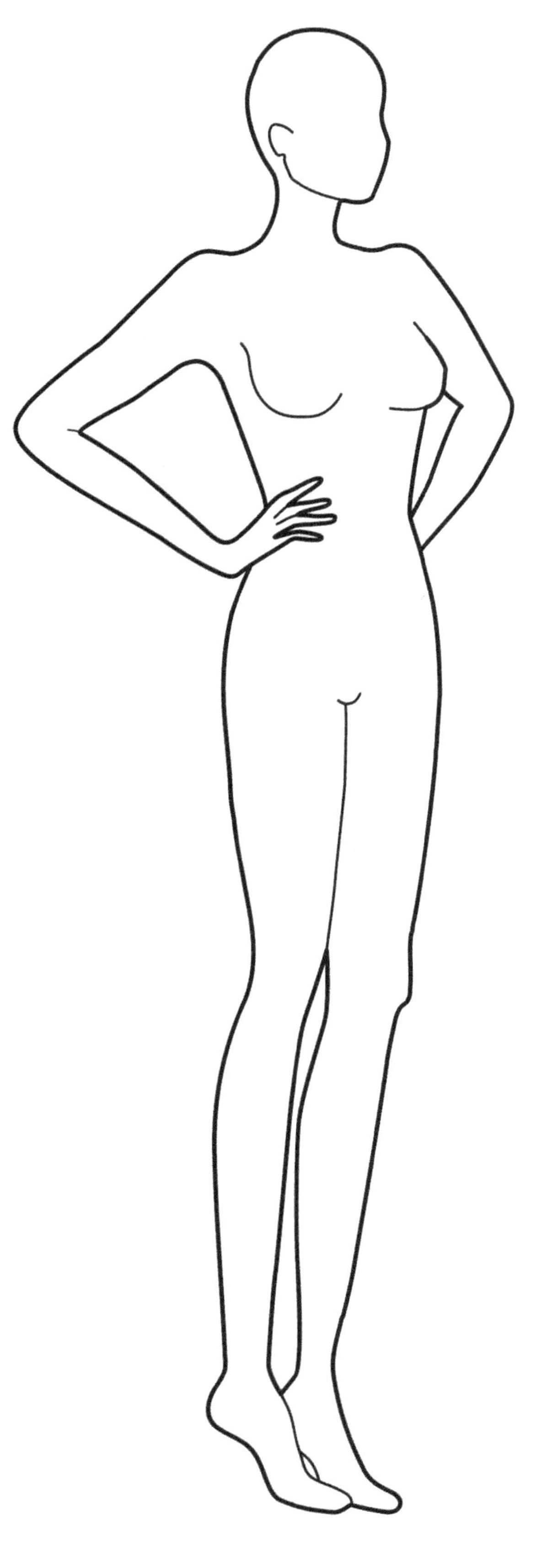
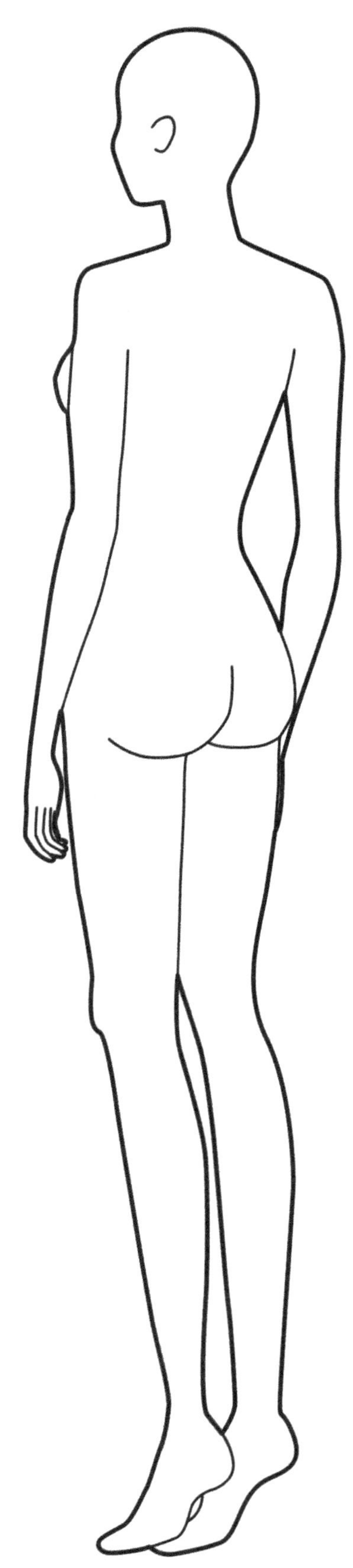

Your Notes & Inspiration Photos

This page is your creative gallery. Use it to track your progress, capture your favorite designs, and reflect on your journey.

- Add sketches, inspiration photos, or cutouts to bring your fashion ideas to life!
- Write down details such as colors, fabrics, or outfit elements that inspired you.
- Leave space for your future self to revisit and compare how your style evolves.

Pro Tip: *A single image or swatch can spark a whole collection. Don't be afraid to save even the smallest details that inspire you!*

Outfit Inspiration:
Office Chic and Runway Glam

Modern Feminine and Futuristic Elegance

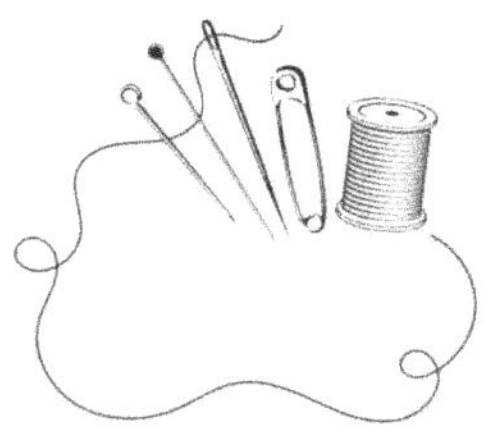

Office Chic Inspiration

Update classic office staples with feminine touches. A blouse with soft ruffles, a skirt with pleats, or trousers in pastel tones bring freshness to the workday wardrobe. Pair these with neutral shoes and discreet accessories for balance. The look remains professional but distinctly personal.

Runway Glam Inspiration

Futuristic elegance blends innovation with grace. Think fluid fabrics combined with metallic accents. Dresses with structured bodices and flowing skirts create contrast between rigidity and softness. Accessories like chrome belts or sculptural jewelry complete the high-fashion aesthetic.

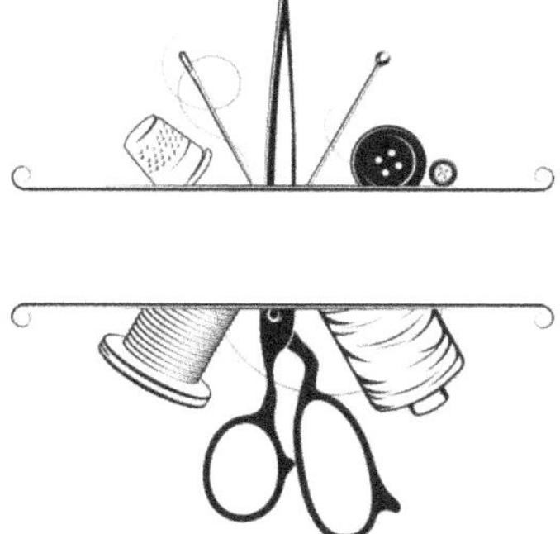

Fashion Practice Guide & Notes

Every sketch is a chance to refine proportions. This page is your training ground for body balance and clothing fit.

How to Use This Page:

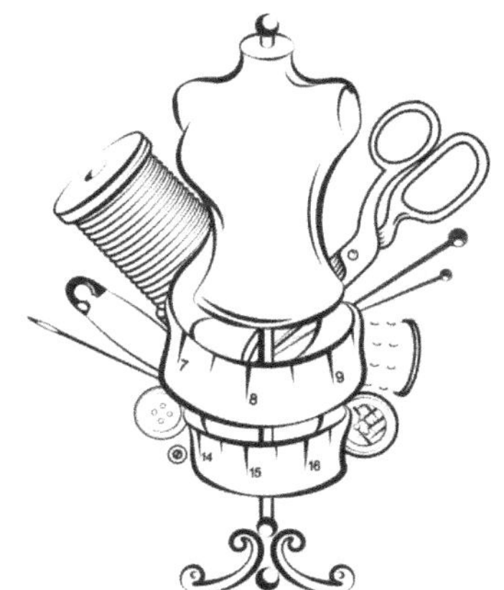

- Focus on body ratios (length of torso, legs, arms).
- Adjust how clothes fall naturally on the figure.
- Add notes on fit: loose, tailored, oversized.

Reflection & Notes:

- Was I accurate in proportion today?
- Which part of the sketch feels most balanced?
- How can I improve next time?

Pro Tip: *Strong proportions are the backbone of great design.*

Outfit Inspiration: Streetwear

The Utility Look

Streetwear often borrows from workwear and military gear. Cargo pants, tactical vests, oversized pockets, and belts with clips bring functionality into fashion.

Colors often lean towards khaki, olive green, black, or camo prints. Accessories like combat boots, bucket hats, or crossbody utility bags finish the look.

Sketch idea: try a cropped tank top styled with oversized cargo pants and a tactical vest. Add chunky boots to complete the utilitarian vibe.

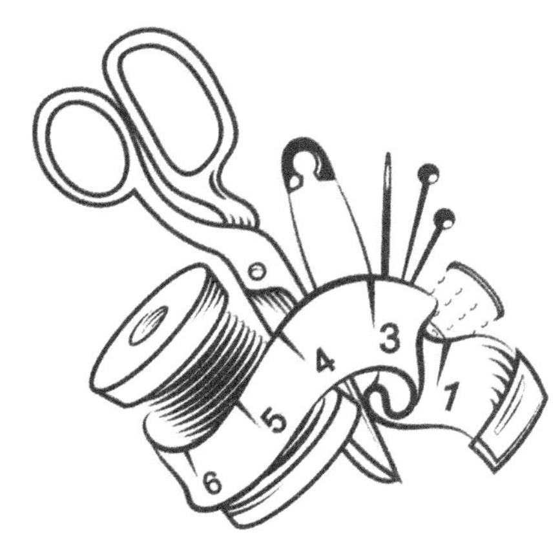

Trends

Inspiration

Textiles

Notes

Details

Swatches

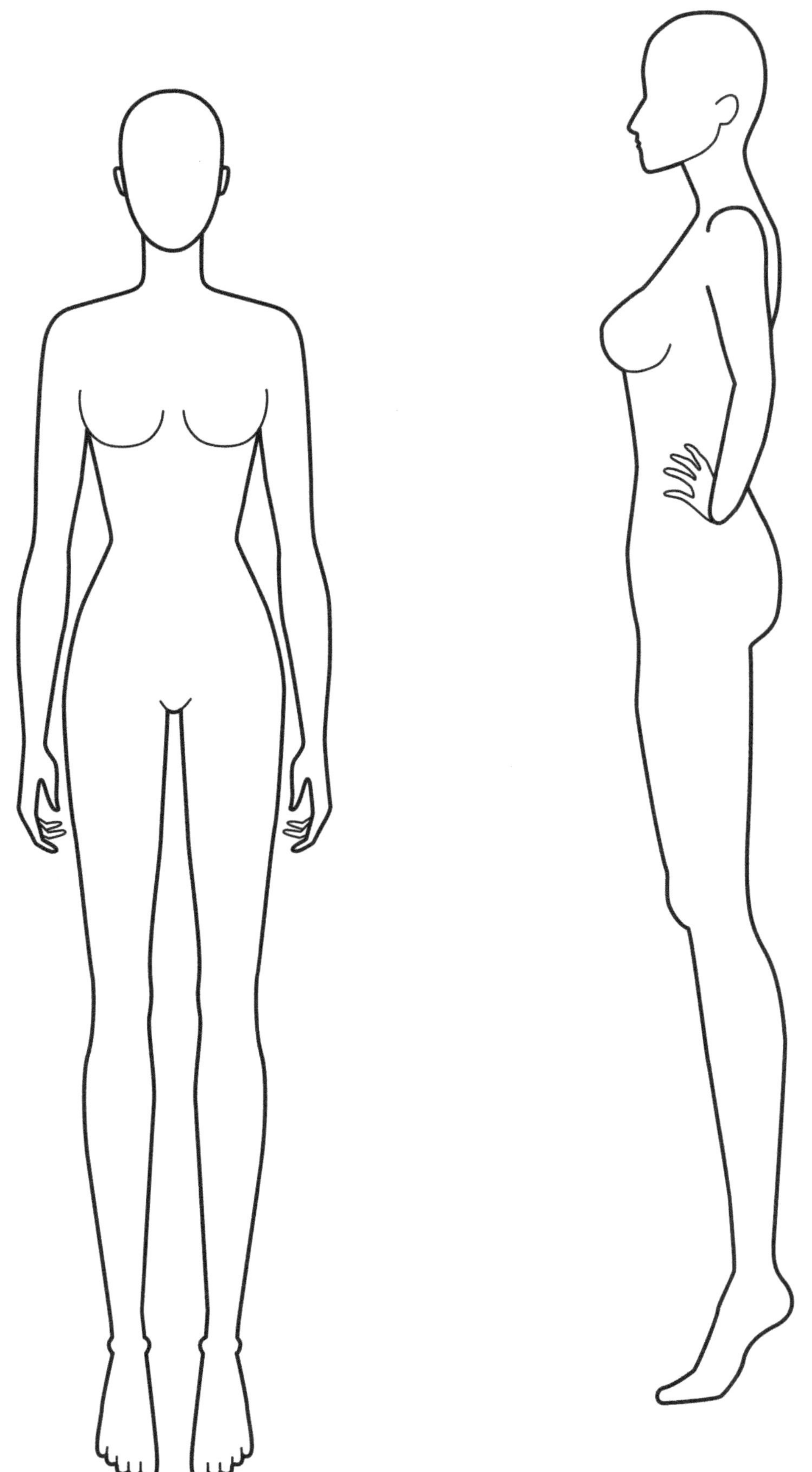

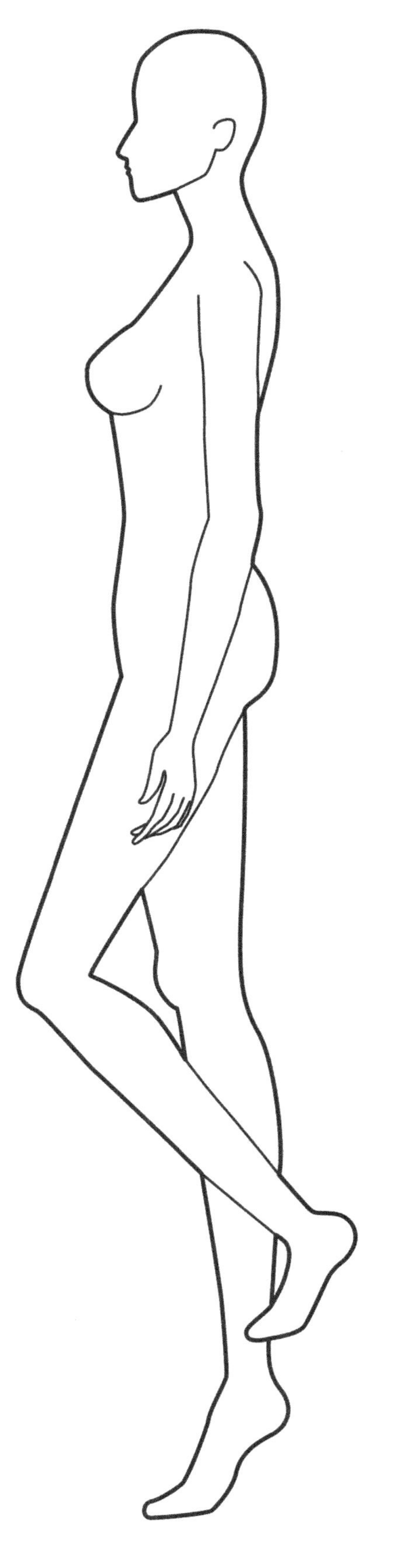
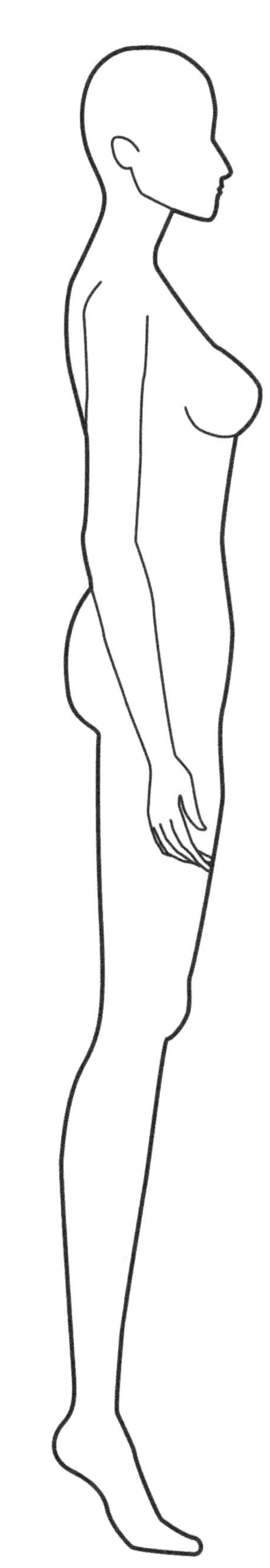

Your Notes & Inspiration Photos

This page is your creative gallery. Use it to track your progress, capture your favorite designs, and reflect on your journey.

- Add sketches, inspiration photos, or cutouts to bring your fashion ideas to life!
- Write down details such as colors, fabrics, or outfit elements that inspired you.
- Leave space for your future self to revisit and compare how your style evolves.

Pro Tip: *A single image or swatch can spark a whole collection. Don't be afraid to save even the smallest details that inspire you!*

Outfit Inspiration: Office Chic and Runway Glam

Smart-Casual Balance and Festival Sparkle

Office Chic Inspiration

Smart-casual is the sweet spot for many offices. Pair cigarette pants with a knit top or a tucked-in blouse. Add a cropped blazer for polish, and finish with flats or ankle boots. This balance works well for creative meetings or days when comfort is essential.

Runway Glam Inspiration

Festival glam thrives on sparkle. Sequins, glitter, and holographic fabrics dominate. Layered skirts, crop tops with embellishments, and bold color palettes embody the celebratory energy. Accessories like feathered headpieces or mirrored sunglasses push the look into playful territory.

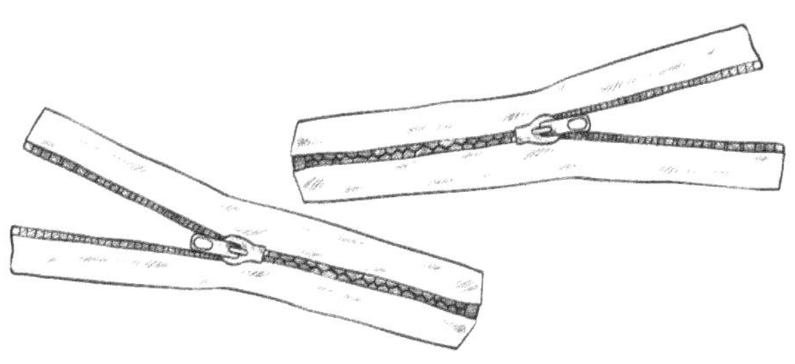

Fashion Practice Guide & Notes

Colors create mood. Use this page to experiment with different palettes and see how they transform the same design.

How to Use This Page:
- Sketch one outfit and apply 2–3 different color schemes.
- Label color choices (warm, cool, monochrome).
- Note how the vibe changes with each palette.

Reflection & Notes:
- Which palette expressed my idea best?
- Did the colors harmonize or clash?
- How would I use this palette again?

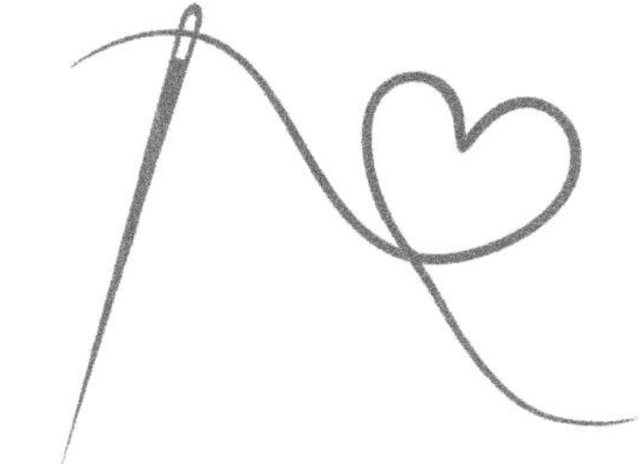

Pro Tip: *The right palette makes your design unforgettable.*

____

____

____

____

____

____

____

____

____

Outfit Inspiration: Streetwear

Vintage Streetwear Revival

Streetwear often reworks fashion from past decades – especially the 80s, 90s, and early 2000s. Oversized denim jackets, tie-dye tees, plaid shirts, or bucket hats all make a comeback.

Design challenge: recreate a vintage-inspired look, but give it a modern twist. Maybe a tie-dye hoodie with modern sneakers, or wide-leg jeans with a crop top and statement sunglasses.

Pro Tip: Streetwear is cyclical – what was "outdated" yesterday is the hottest trend today.

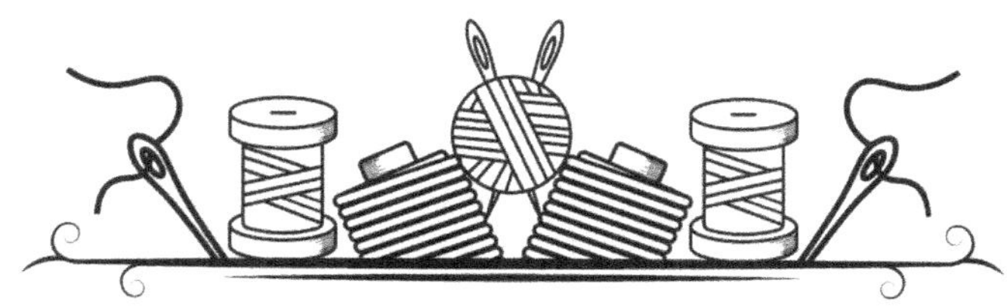

Trends

Inspiration

Textiles

Notes

Details

Swatches

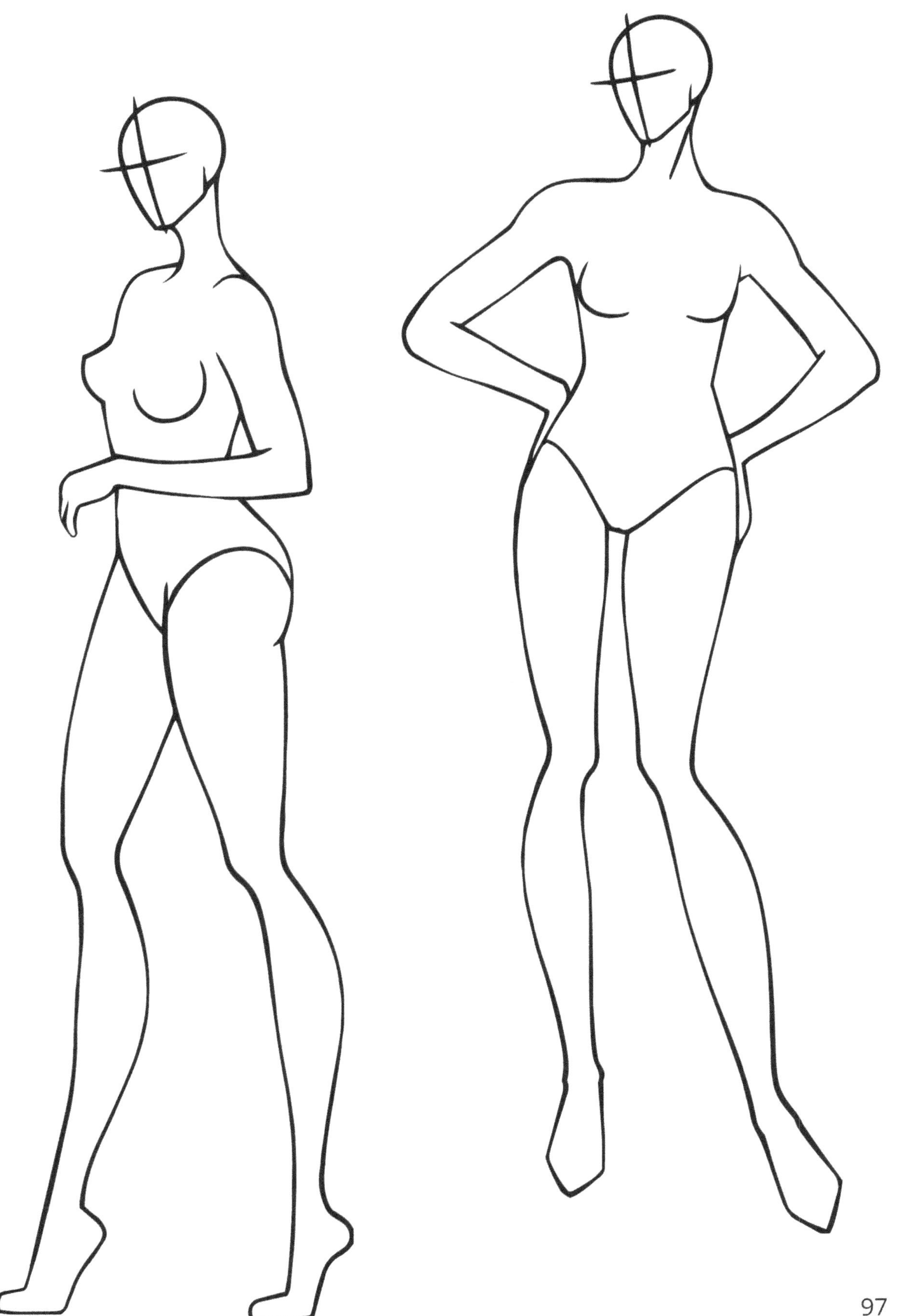

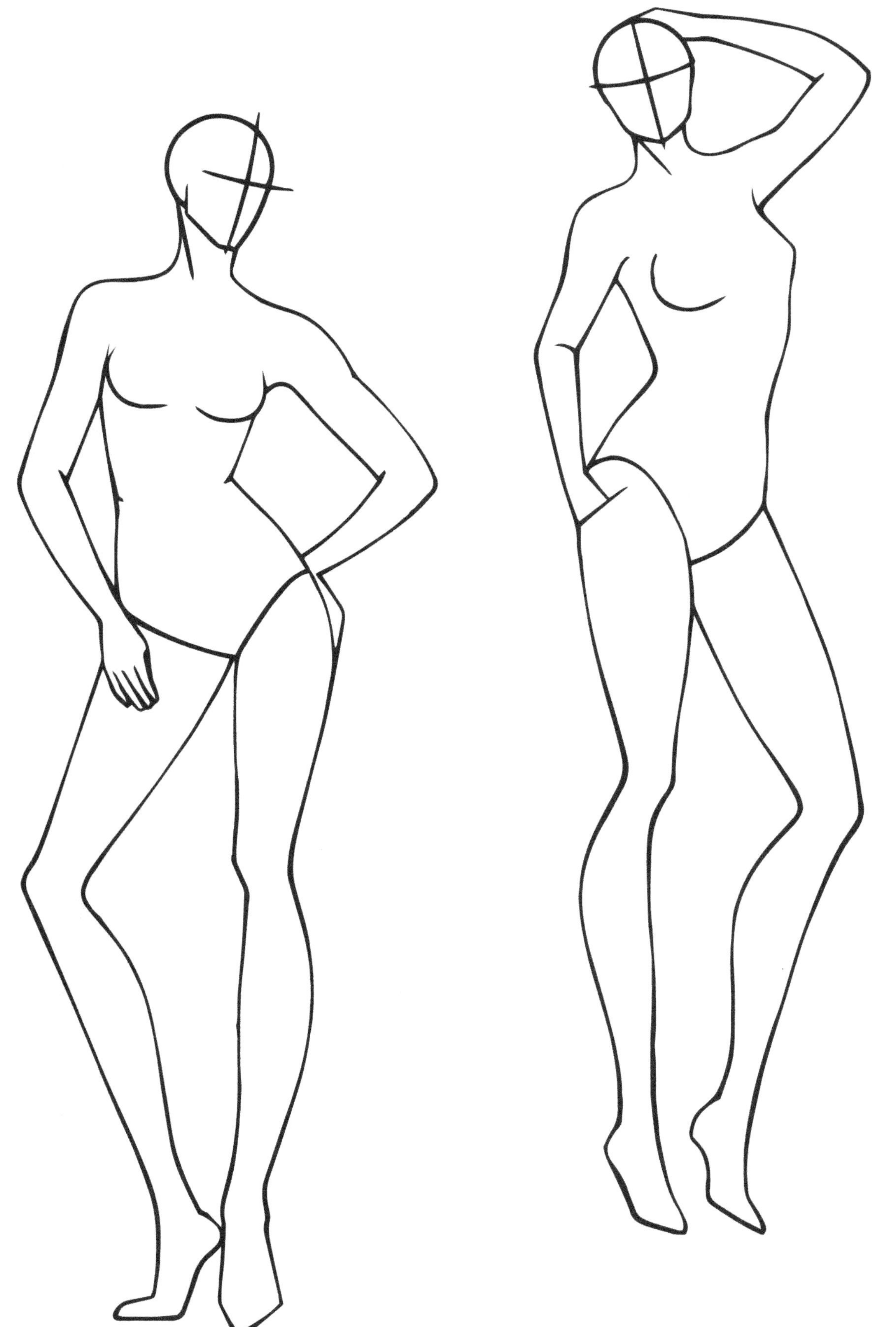

Your Notes & Inspiration Photos

This page is your creative gallery. Use it to track your progress, capture your favorite designs, and reflect on your journey.

- Add sketches, inspiration photos, or cutouts to bring your fashion ideas to life!
- Write down details such as colors, fabrics, or outfit elements that inspired you.
- Leave space for your future self to revisit and compare how your style evolves.

Pro Tip: *A single image or swatch can spark a whole collection. Don't be afraid to save even the smallest details that inspire you!*

Outfit Inspiration:
Office Chic and Runway Glam

Elegant Office Dress and Sustainable Couture

Office Chic Inspiration

An elegant office dress simplifies mornings while keeping style intact. A knee-length sheath dress in a solid color paired with a cropped jacket works perfectly. Choose soft fabrics that move comfortably while maintaining structure. Neutral shoes and a slim belt complete the look.

Runway Glam Inspiration

Sustainable couture explores luxury with a conscience. Designers experiment with natural silk, bamboo fabrics, or recycled embellishments. Full-length gowns with minimal waste patterns emphasize beauty and innovation. Highlighting ethical fashion choices on the runway inspires both awareness and admiration.

Fashion Practice Guide & Notes

Outfits are stronger in collections. Use this page to think beyond one design and sketch pieces that work together.

How to Use This Page:

- Design 2–3 variations of the same theme.
- Keep one unifying detail (color, fabric, silhouette).
- Add notes about how they fit in a capsule wardrobe.

Reflection & Notes:

- Did my sketches feel like part of one collection?
- Which piece stands out most?
- How could I refine the harmony between them?

Pro Tip: *Strong collections come from consistency with a twist.*

Outfit Inspiration: Streetwear

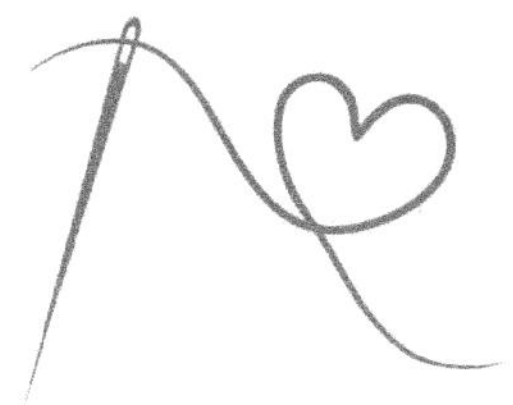

Sneakers at the Center

Sneakers are more than footwear in streetwear – they're the foundation of an outfit. Sometimes the entire look is built around the shoes.

Design exercise: pick a pair of bold sneakers (imagine them in neon colors, high-top, or chunky soles) and design the entire outfit to match. Maybe oversized joggers tucked into socks, paired with a cropped hoodie and layered bomber.

Fabric tip: balance bold sneakers with neutral clothing, or match details (laces, stripes) with accessories for cohesion.

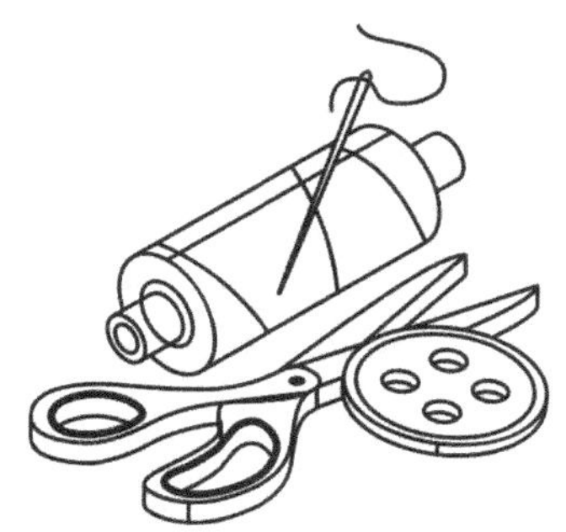

Trends

Inspiration

Textiles

Notes

Details

Swatches

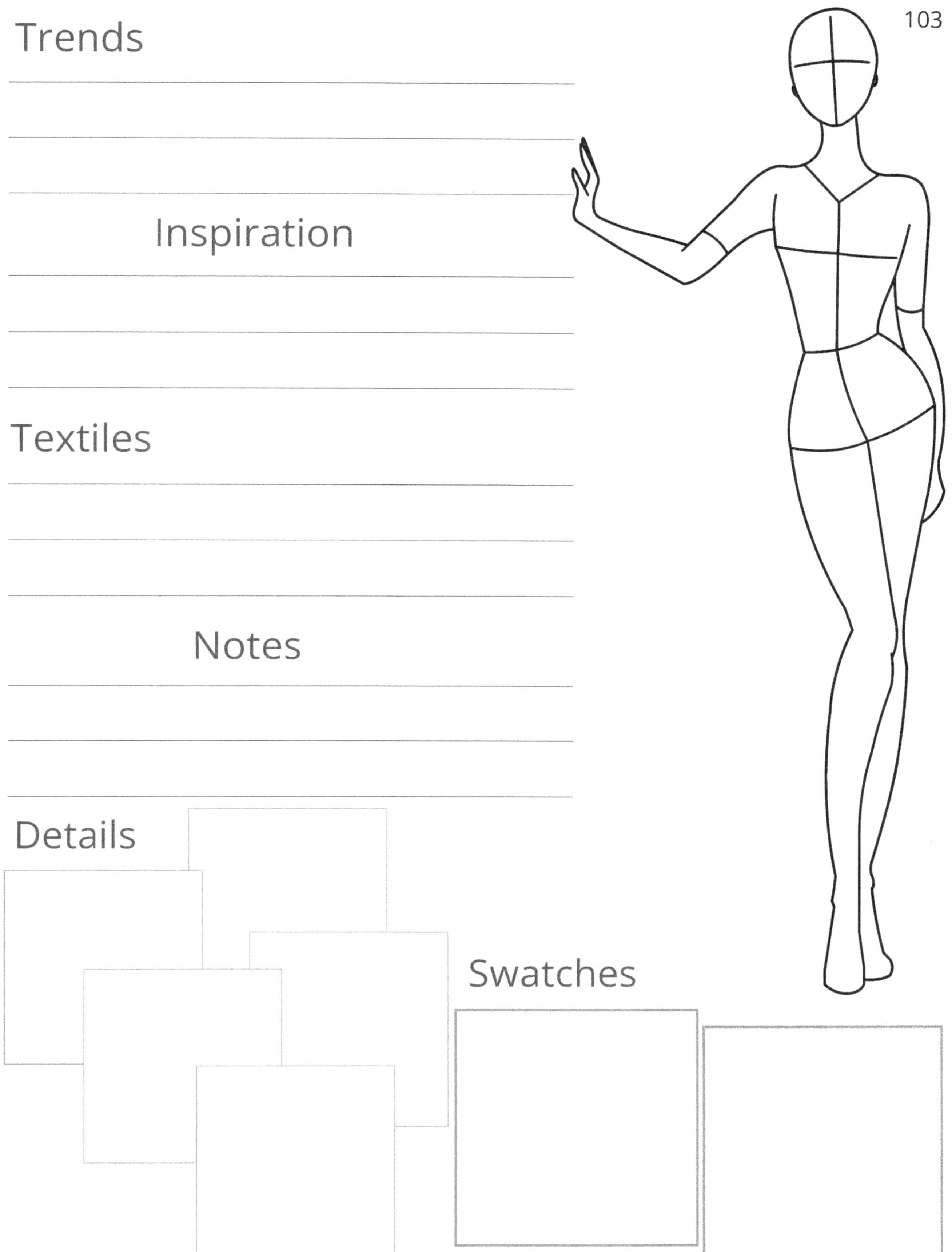

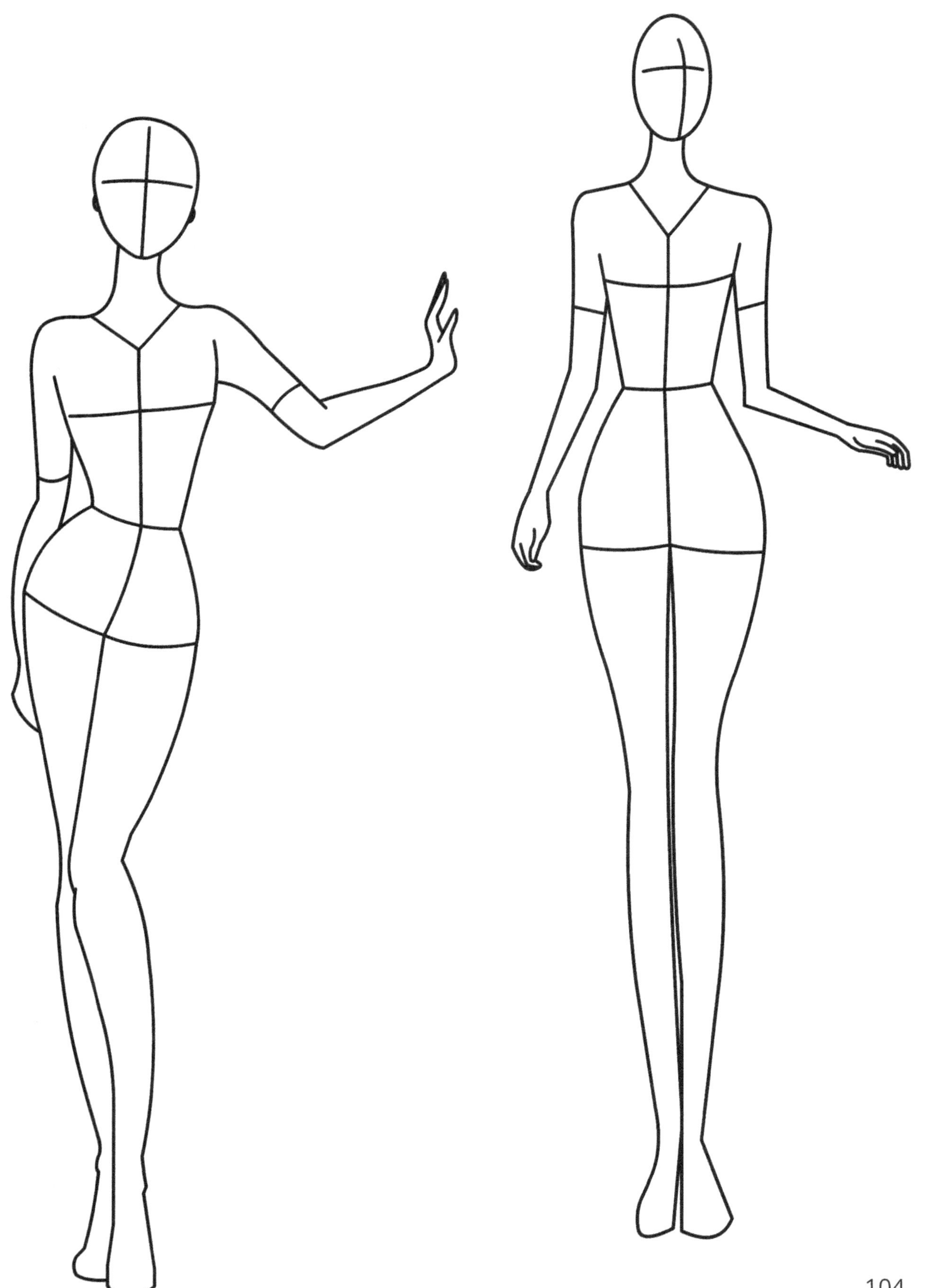

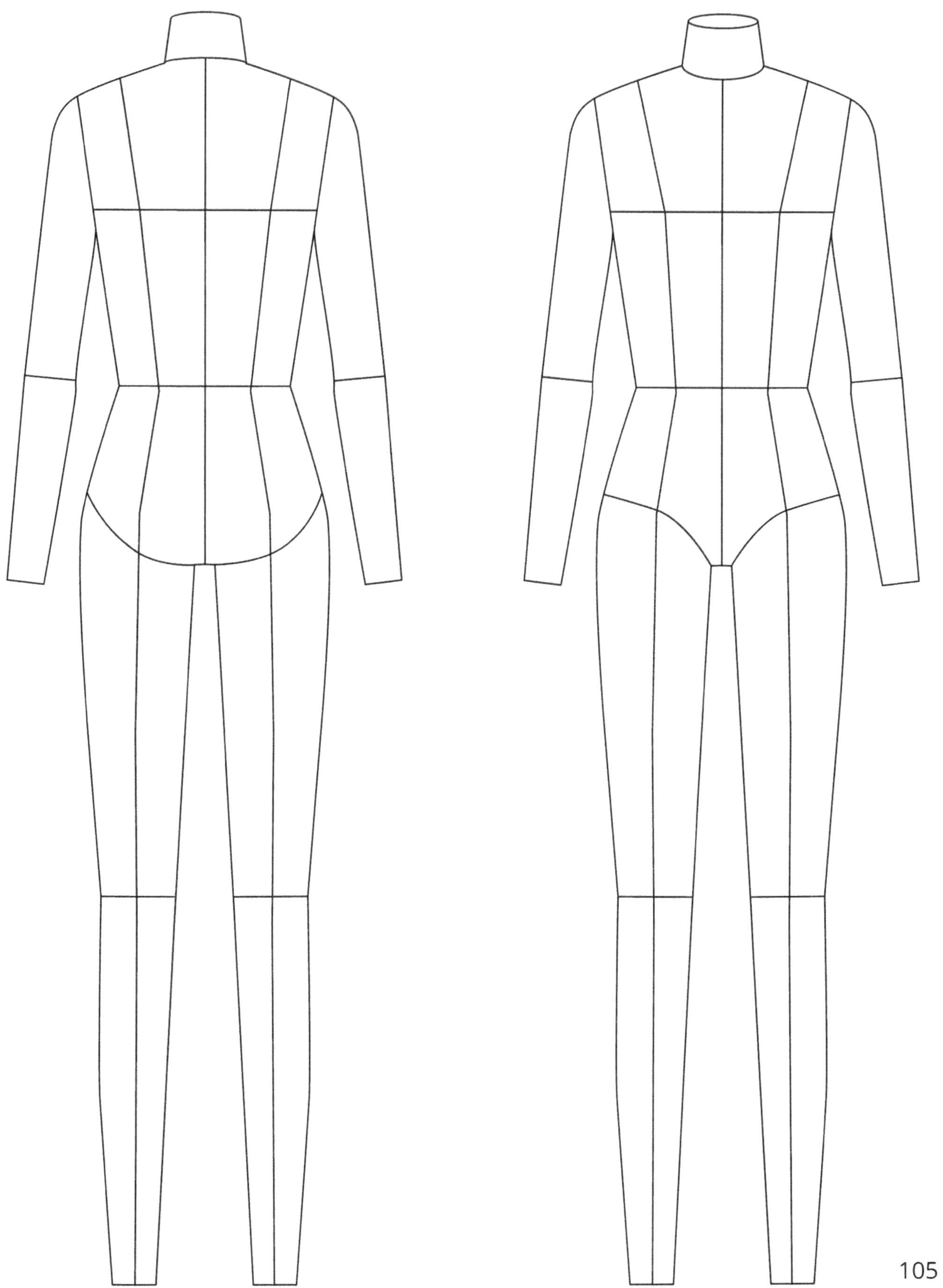

Your Notes & Inspiration Photos

This page is your creative gallery. Use it to track your progress, capture your favorite designs, and reflect on your journey.

- Add sketches, inspiration photos, or cutouts to bring your fashion ideas to life!
- Write down details such as colors, fabrics, or outfit elements that inspired you.
- Leave space for your future self to revisit and compare how your style evolves.

Pro Tip: *A single image or swatch can spark a whole collection. Don't be afraid to save even the smallest details that inspire you!*

Outfit Inspiration: Office Chic and Runway Glam

Trend-Adaptive Office Look and Futuristic Showstopper

Office Chic Inspiration

Adapting subtle trends into office wear keeps the wardrobe current. Wide-leg trousers, muted pastels, or oversized blazers can be styled professionally when balanced with neutrals. Accessories such as a structured crossbody bag or modern loafers keep the look grounded.

Runway Glam Inspiration

A futuristic showstopper demands boldness. Dresses with LED details, reflective fabrics, or sculptural silhouettes redefine fashion boundaries. These are statement-making pieces designed to wow audiences and inspire conversation.

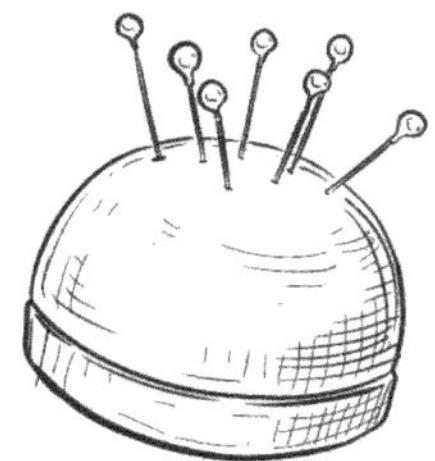

Fashion Practice Guide & Notes

Sometimes less is more. Use this page to test minimalism: clean lines, few details, and a focus on silhouette.

How to Use This Page:
- Sketch an outfit with no more than 3 key elements.
- Focus on proportion and negative space.
- Note how simplicity changes the vibe.

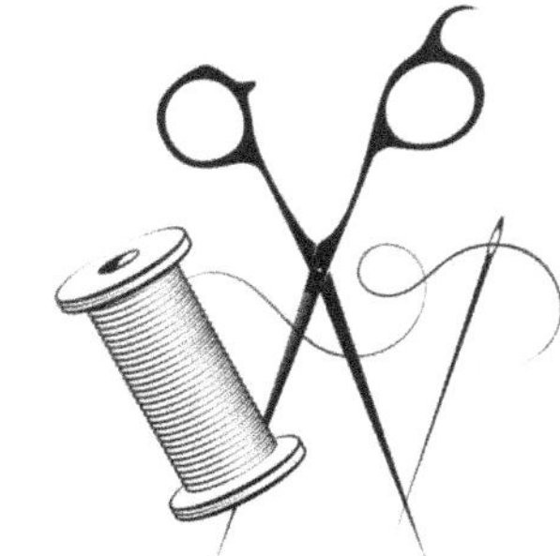

Reflection & Notes:
- Did simplicity make the design stronger?
- Which detail carries the most weight?
- What would I remove or keep next time?

Pro Tip*: Minimalism can speak louder than excess.*

Outfit Inspiration: Streetwear

Streetwear Accessories that Pop

Accessories often define streetwear. Bucket hats, oversized sunglasses, chunky chains, fanny packs, and beanies are the finishing touches that make an outfit memorable.

Sketch challenge: design a simple base outfit, then elevate it with 2–3 bold accessories. Notice how accessories can transform minimal clothing into a complete streetwear look.

Pro Tip: *Accessories are the fastest way to experiment with trends without changing the whole outfit.*

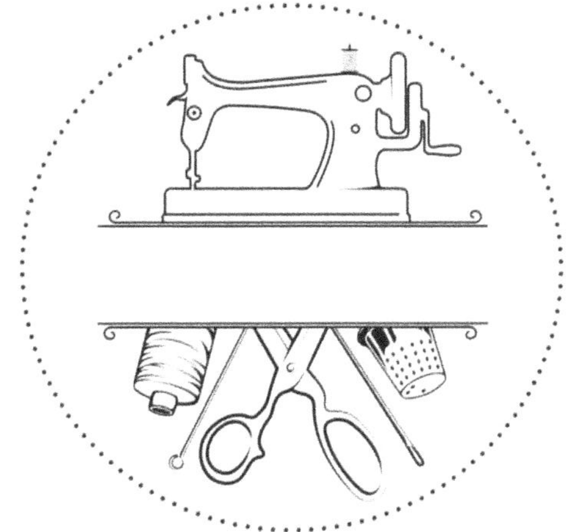

Trends

Inspiration

Textiles

Notes

Details

Swatches

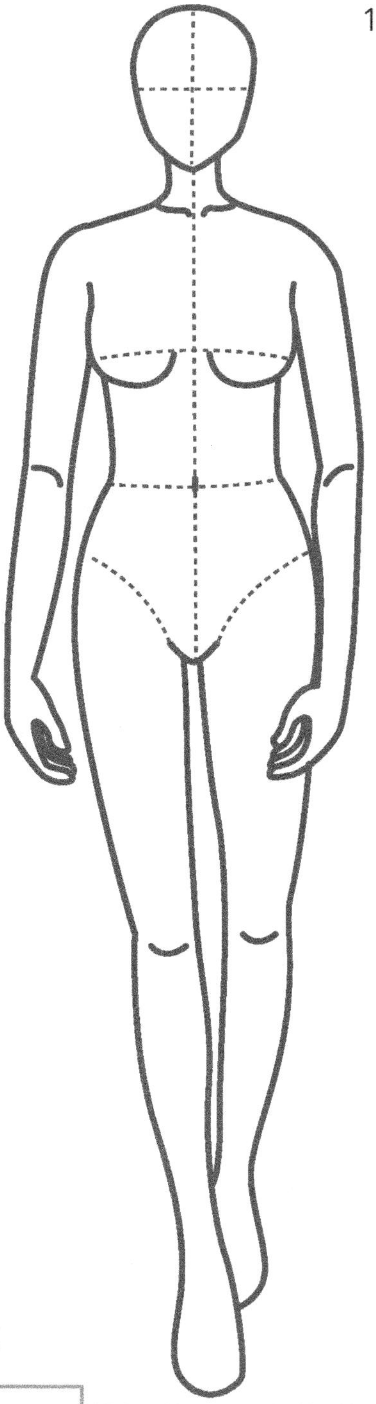

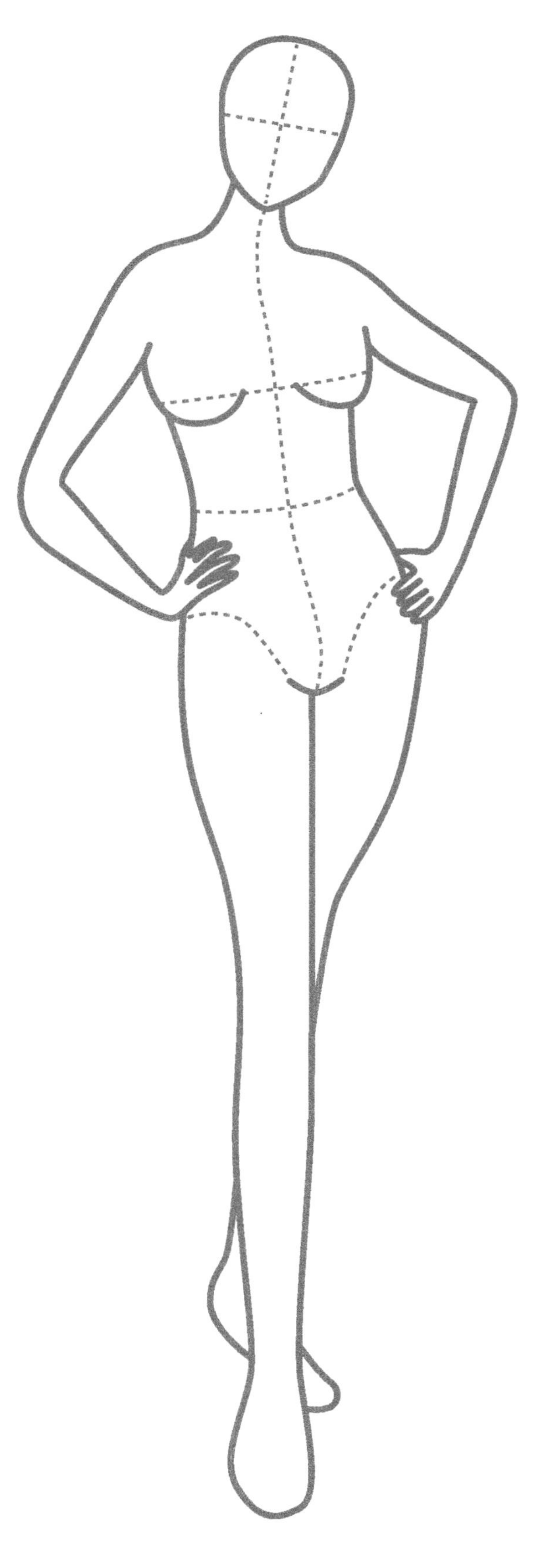
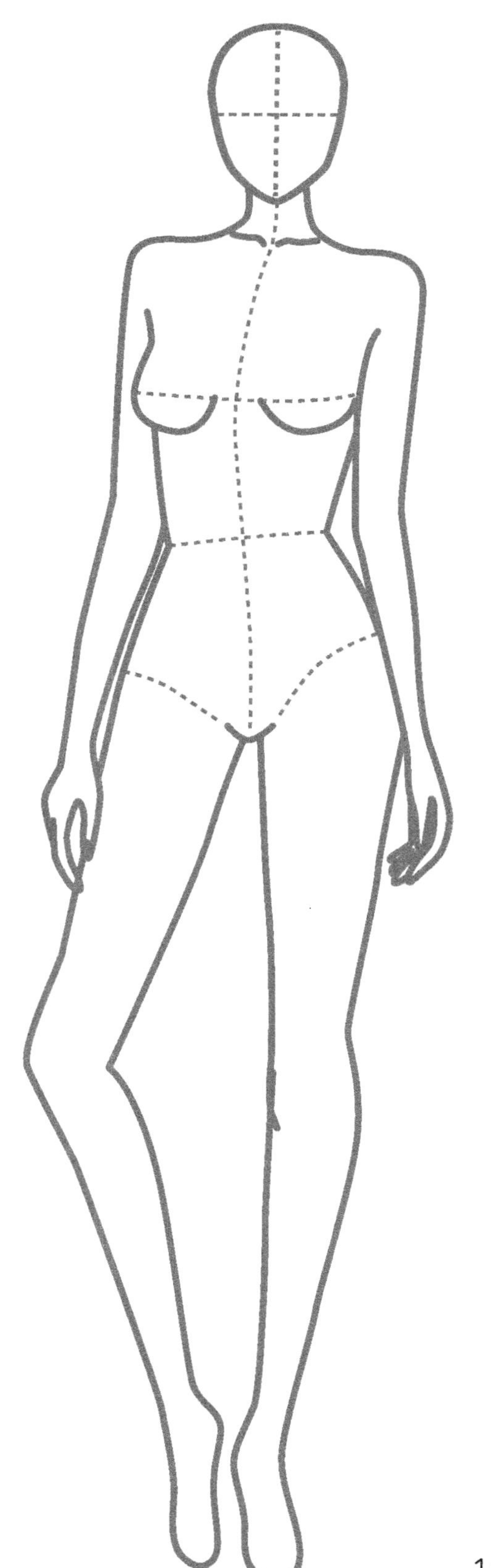

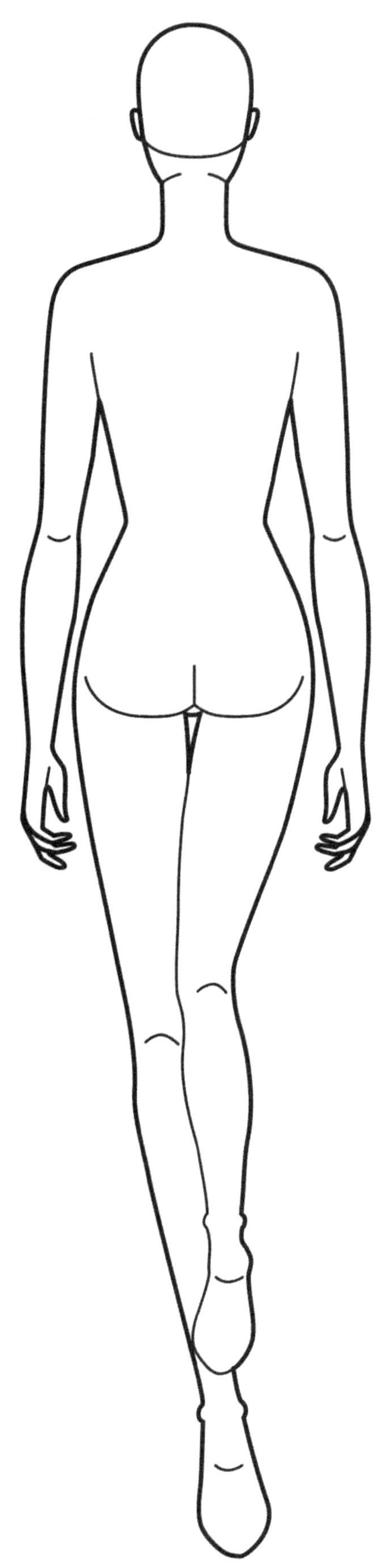
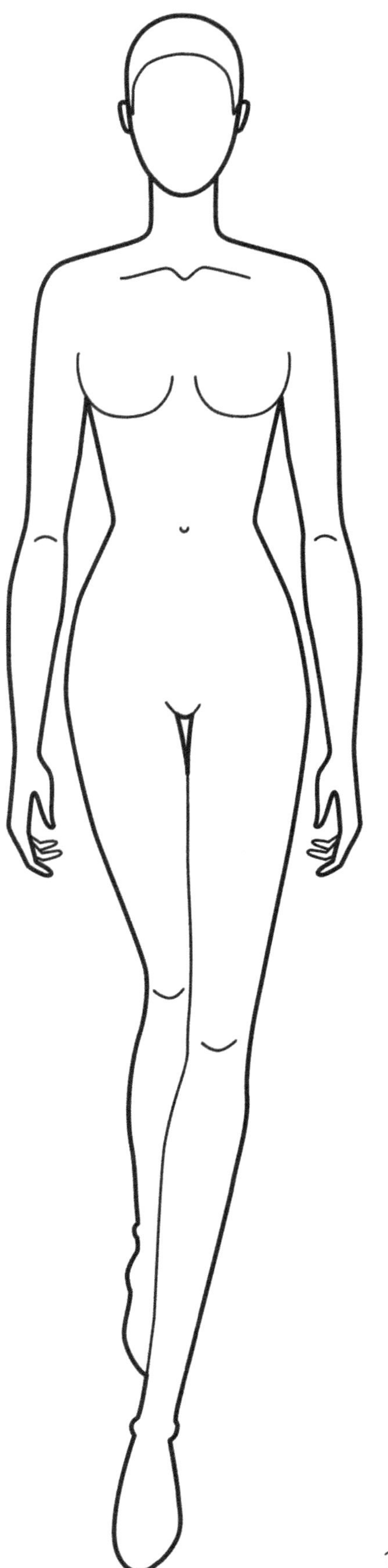

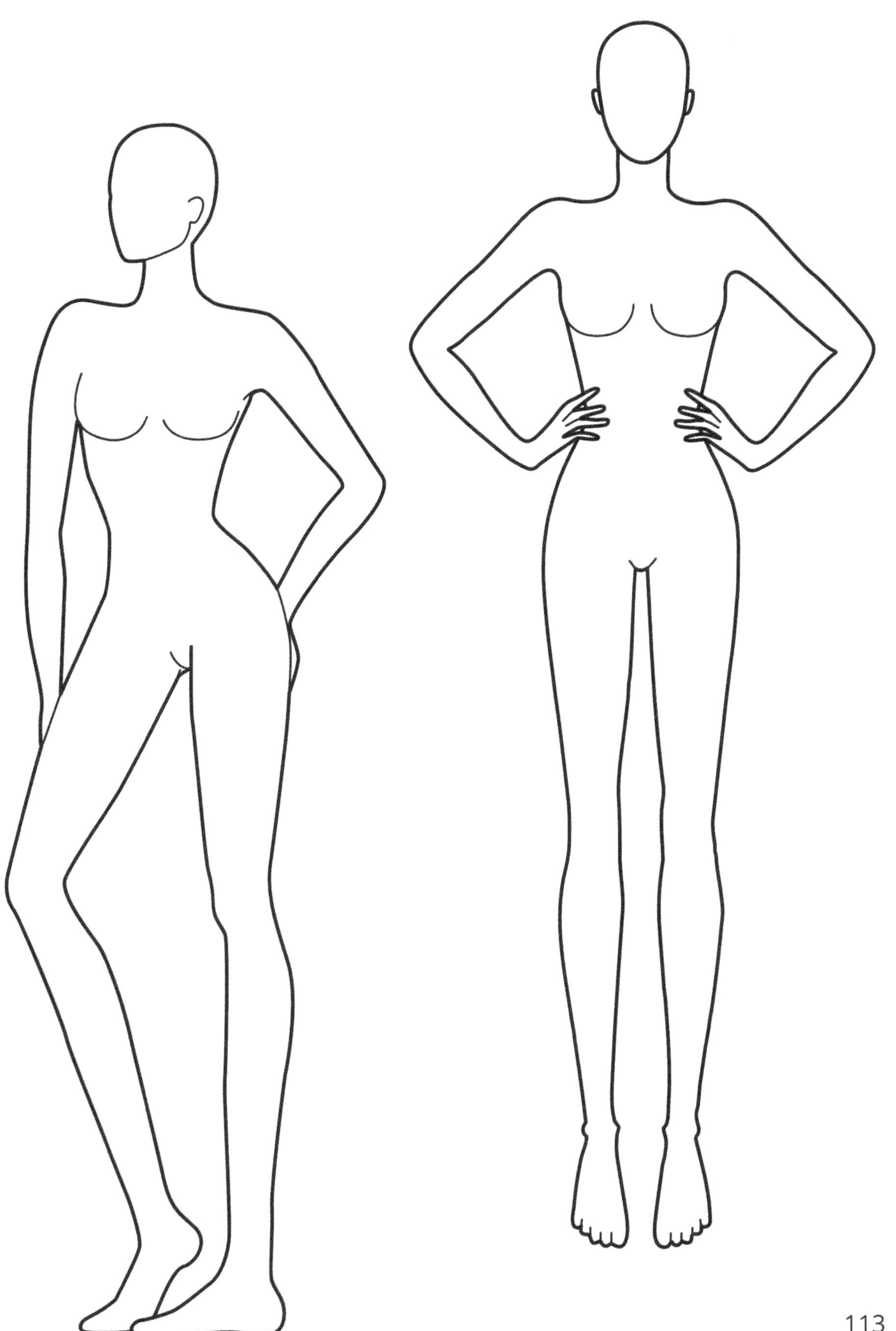

Your Notes & Inspiration Photos

This page is your creative gallery. Use it to track your progress, capture your favorite designs, and reflect on your journey.

- Add sketches, inspiration photos, or cutouts to bring your fashion ideas to life!
- Write down details such as colors, fabrics, or outfit elements that inspired you.
- Leave space for your future self to revisit and compare how your style evolves.

Pro Tip: *A single image or swatch can spark a whole collection. Don't be afraid to save even the smallest details that inspire you!*

Outfit Inspiration: Office Chic and Runway Glam

Office Layering and Red Carpet Classic

Office Chic Inspiration

Layering transforms simple office staples into complex, stylish ensembles. Pair a turtleneck under a sleeveless dress, or wear a blouse beneath a structured jumpsuit. Scarves, belts, and blazers add depth without losing professionalism. Smart layering is both practical and chic.

Runway Glam Inspiration

Classic red carpet glam never fails: floor-length gowns, rich velvet or satin fabrics, and elegant draping. Pair with high heels, sleek updos, and sparkling jewelry. The timeless appeal ensures sophistication and elegance at every step.

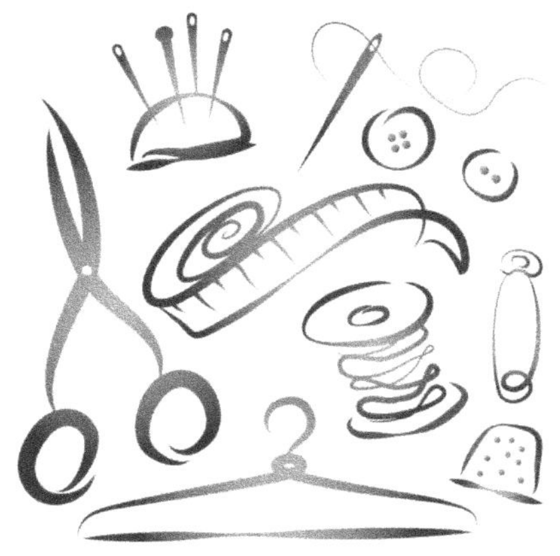

Fashion Practice Guide & Notes

 This page is for reflection and celebration. Look back at your past sketches and see how far you've come. Use it to capture lessons and set your next goal.

How to Use This Page:
- Summarize what you've learned so far.
- Sketch one design that represents your progress.
- Write what you want to explore next.

Reflection & Notes:
- What was my biggest improvement?
- Which technique do I want to master?
- What's my next design challenge?

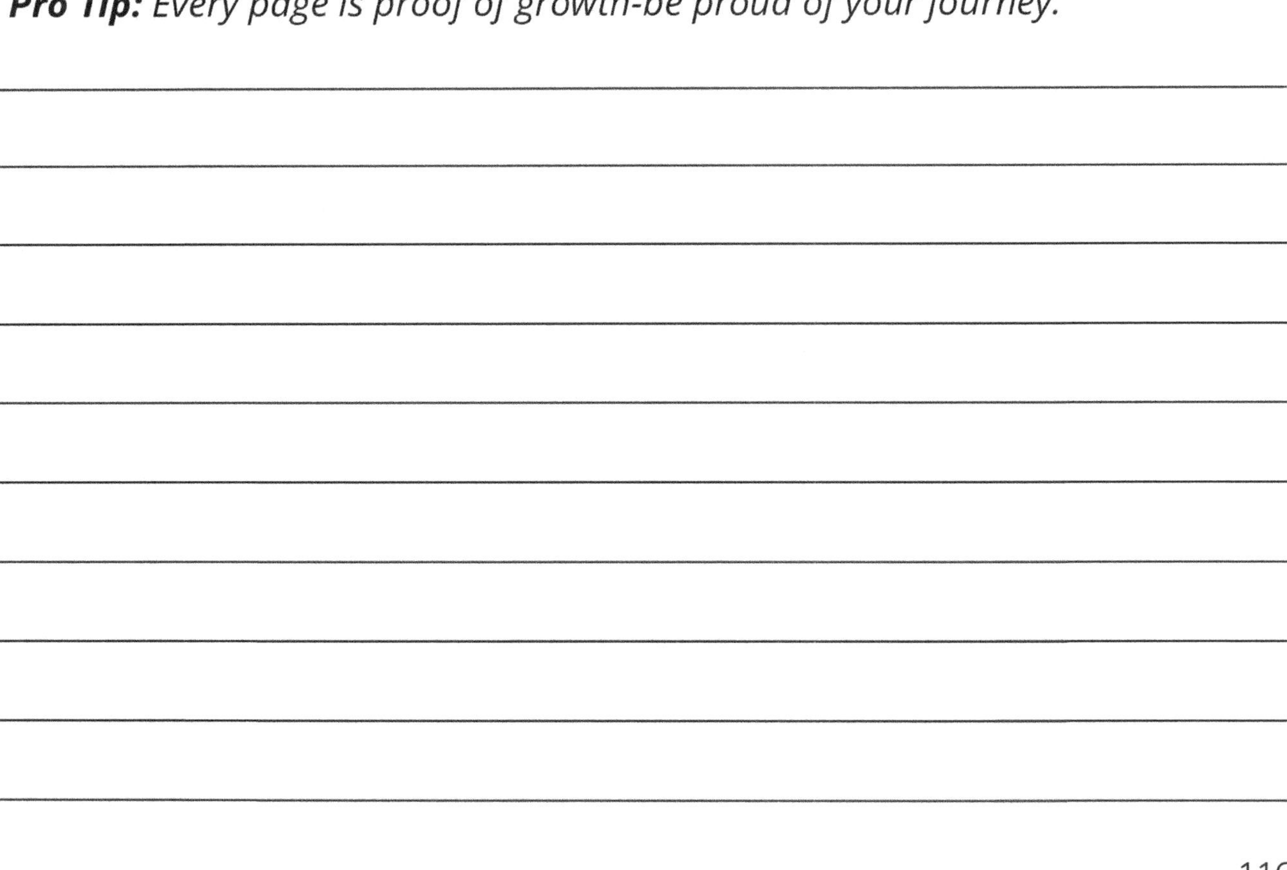

Pro Tip: *Every page is proof of growth-be proud of your journey.*

____

____

____

____

____

____

____

____

Outfit Inspiration: Streetwear

Streetwear as Self-Expression

At its heart, streetwear is about personal identity. It's not about copying trends but about mixing elements to tell your own story. Whether oversized, colorful, minimal, or sporty, the key is authenticity.

Sketch exercise: design an outfit that feels like "you." Think of favorite colors, cuts, or cultural influences. Add details that make the outfit unique – maybe patches, prints, or your own logo idea.

Final thought: *Streetwear is not just clothing – it's an attitude. Confidence is the best accessory you can wear.*

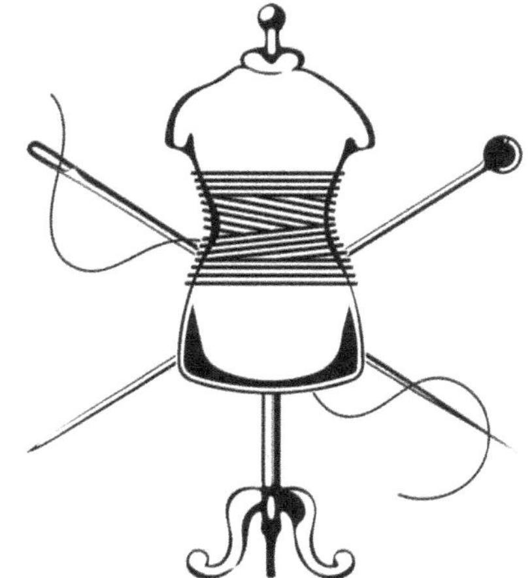

Trends

Inspiration

Textiles

Notes

Details

Swatches

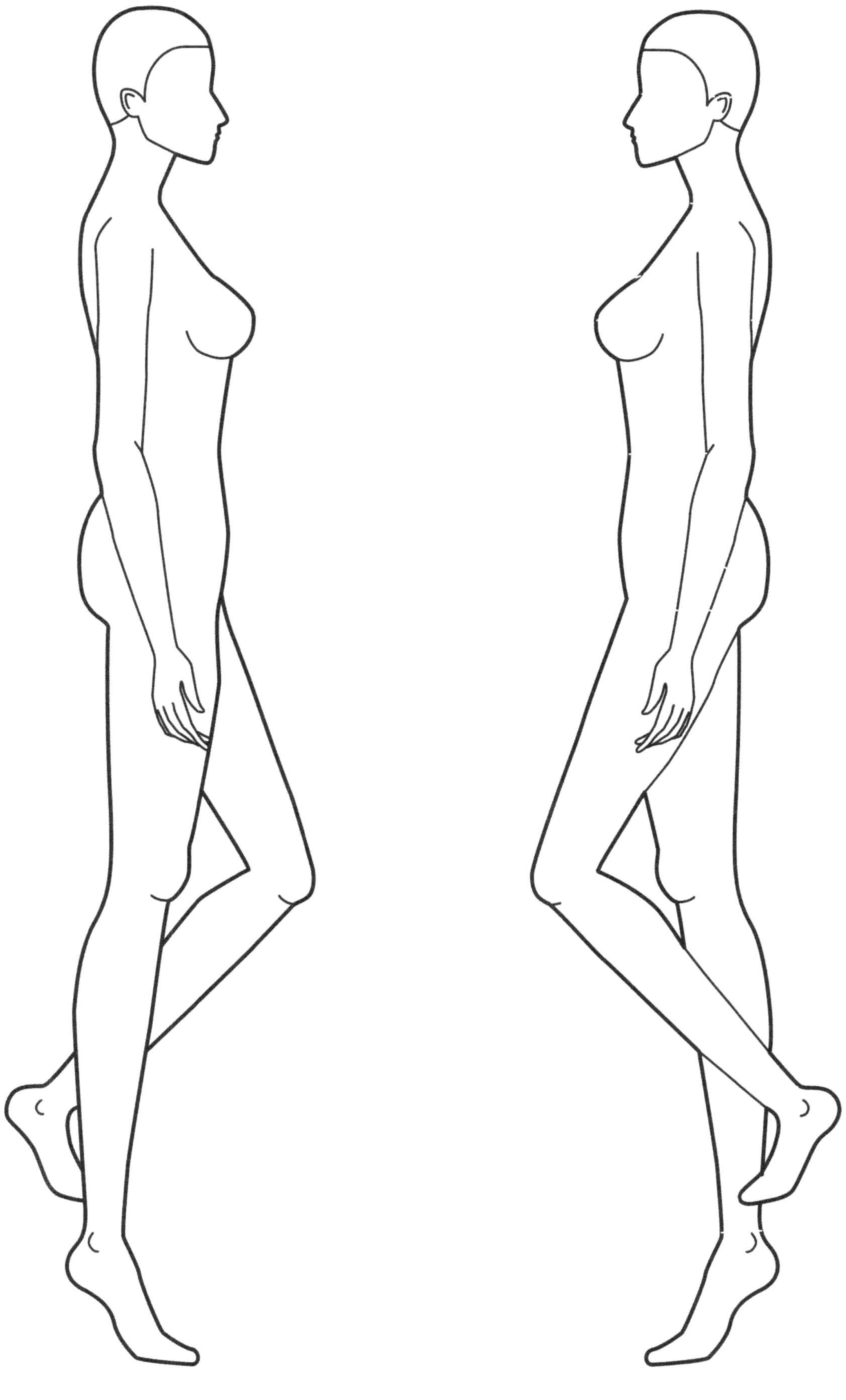

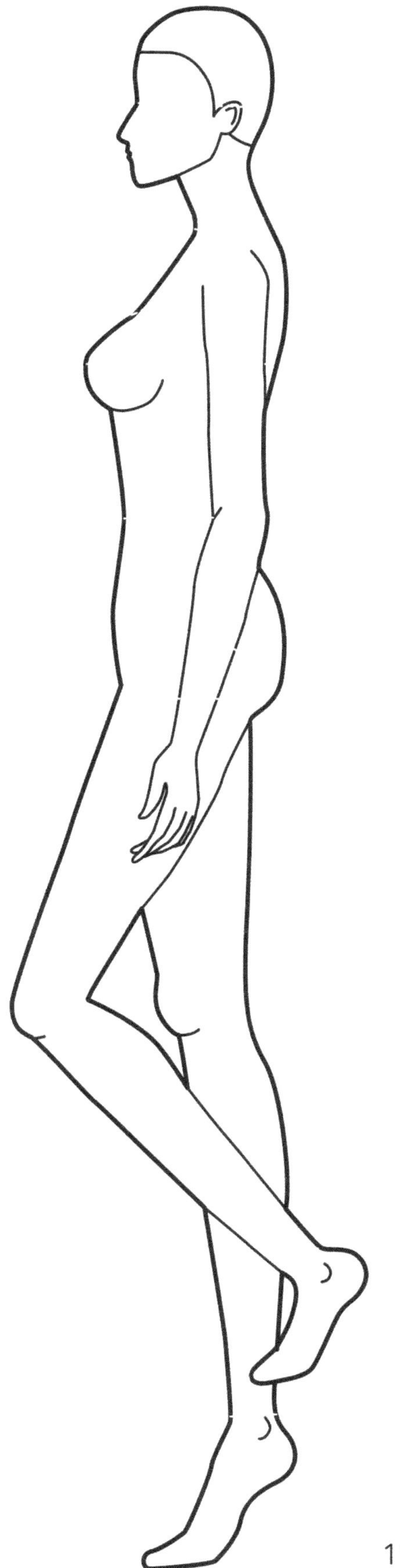

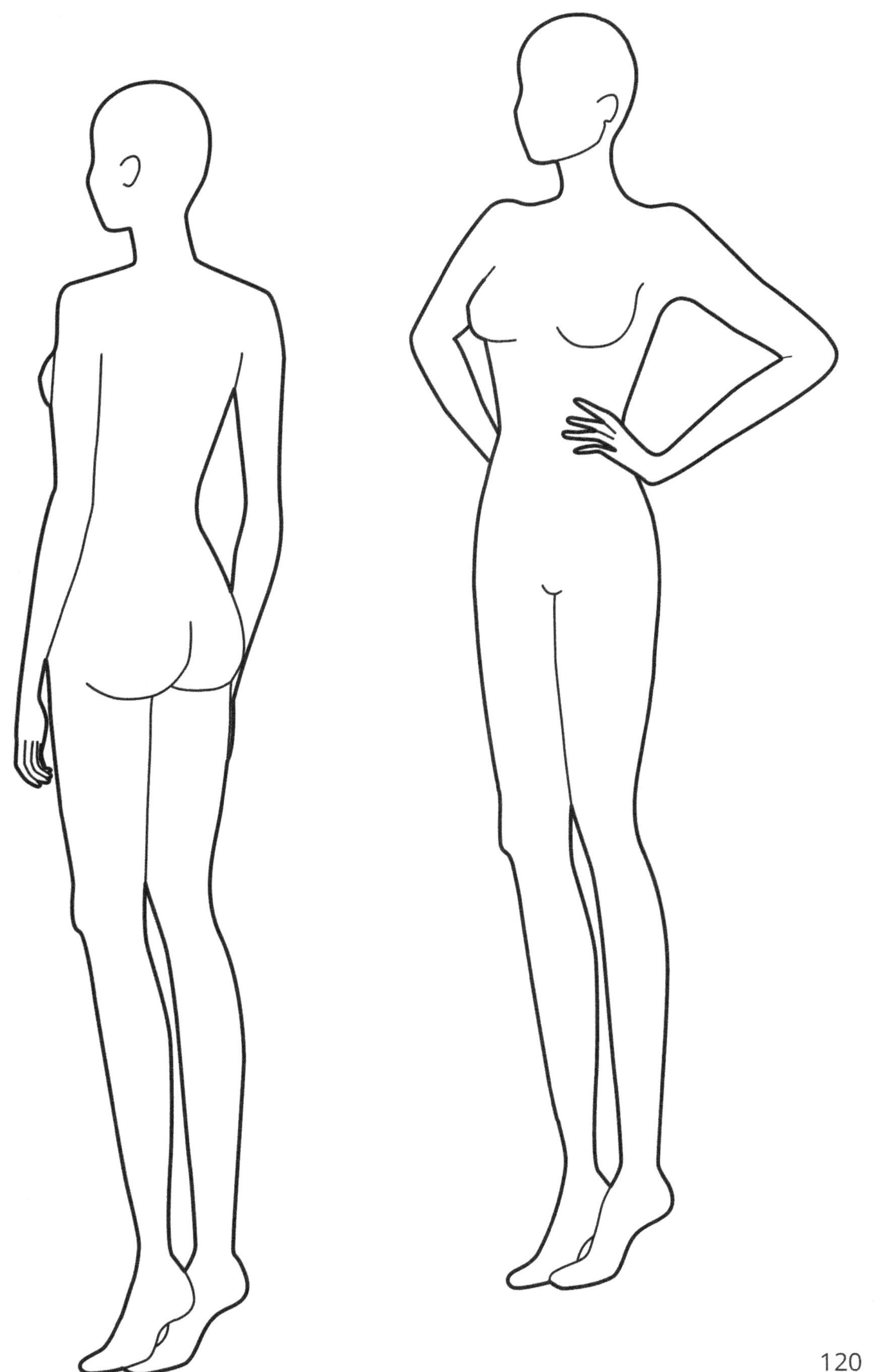

Your Notes & Inspiration Photos

This page is your creative gallery. Use it to track your progress, capture your favorite designs, and reflect on your journey.

- Add sketches, inspiration photos, or cutouts to bring your fashion ideas to life!
- Write down details such as colors, fabrics, or outfit elements that inspired you.
- Leave space for your future self to revisit and compare how your style evolves.

Pro Tip: *A single image or swatch can spark a whole collection. Don't be afraid to save even the smallest details that inspire you!*

Outfit Inspiration: Office Chic and Runway Glam

Bold Office Statement and Avant-Garde Glam

Office Chic Inspiration

Some days call for making a statement. A bold-colored suit – emerald, royal blue, or bright red – exudes confidence. Pair with a neutral blouse and understated shoes to let the suit be the star. This approach works well for presentations or important meetings.

Runway Glam Inspiration

Avant-garde glam challenges tradition. Think exaggerated shapes, layered volumes, or experimental textures. Dresses may combine unconventional fabrics, asymmetrical cuts, or oversized accessories. These runway looks are meant to provoke thought while dazzling audiences.

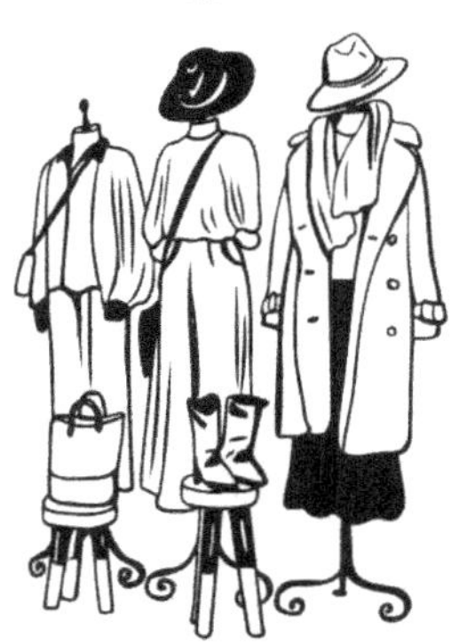

Trends

Inspiration

Textiles

Notes

Details

Swatches

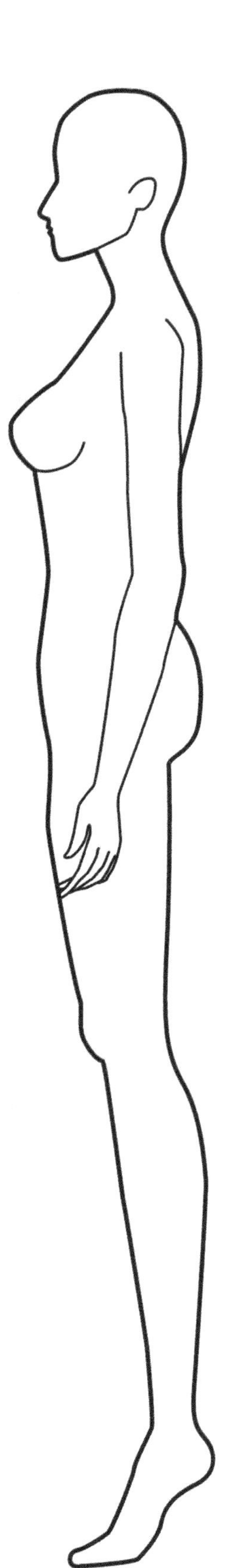
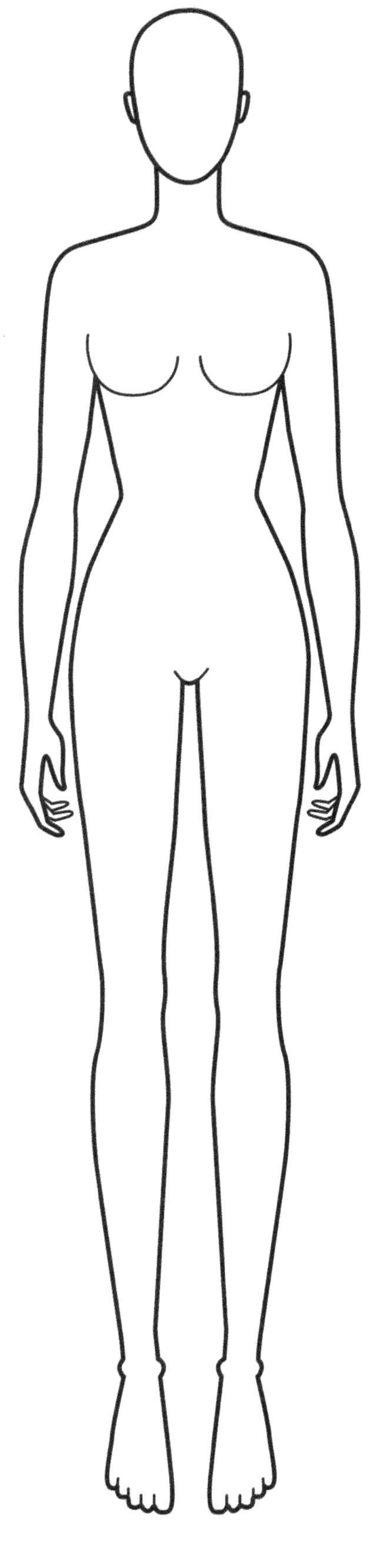

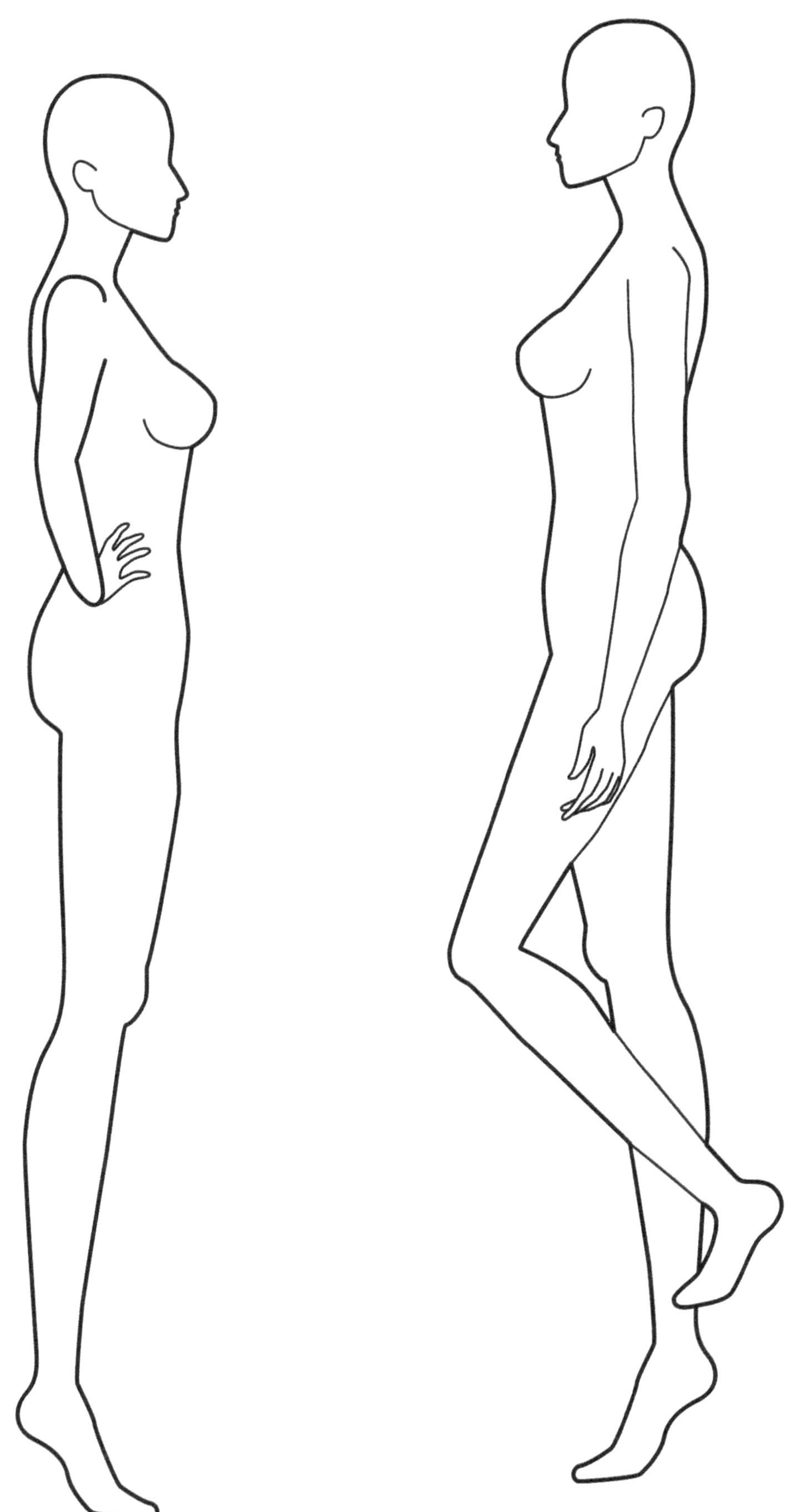

Trends

Inspiration

Textiles

Notes

Details

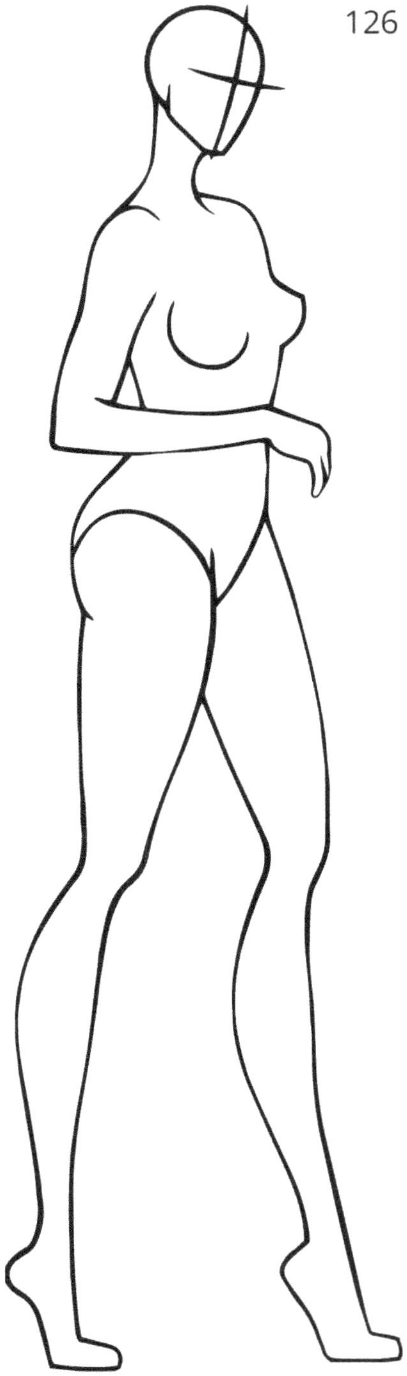

Swatches

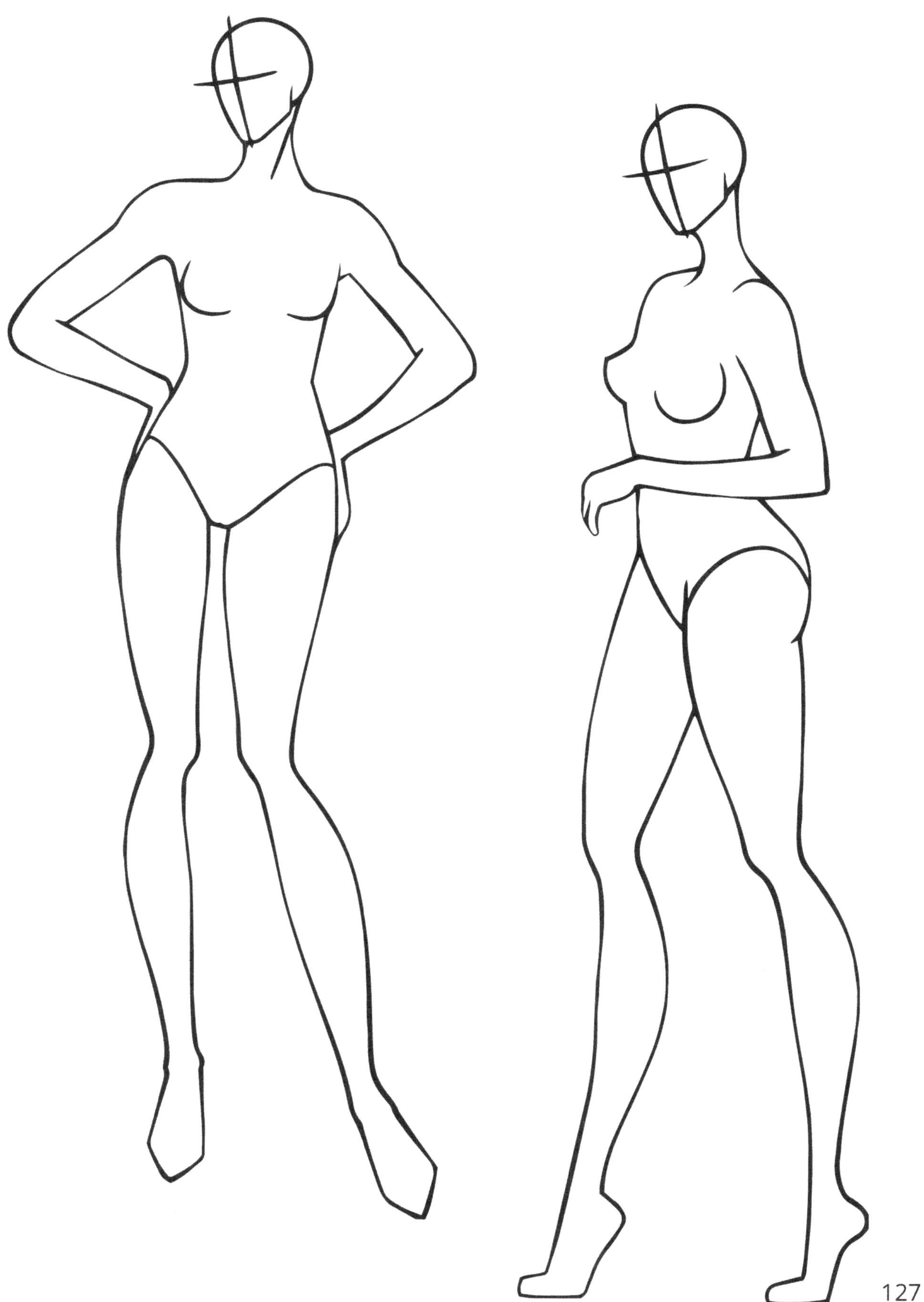

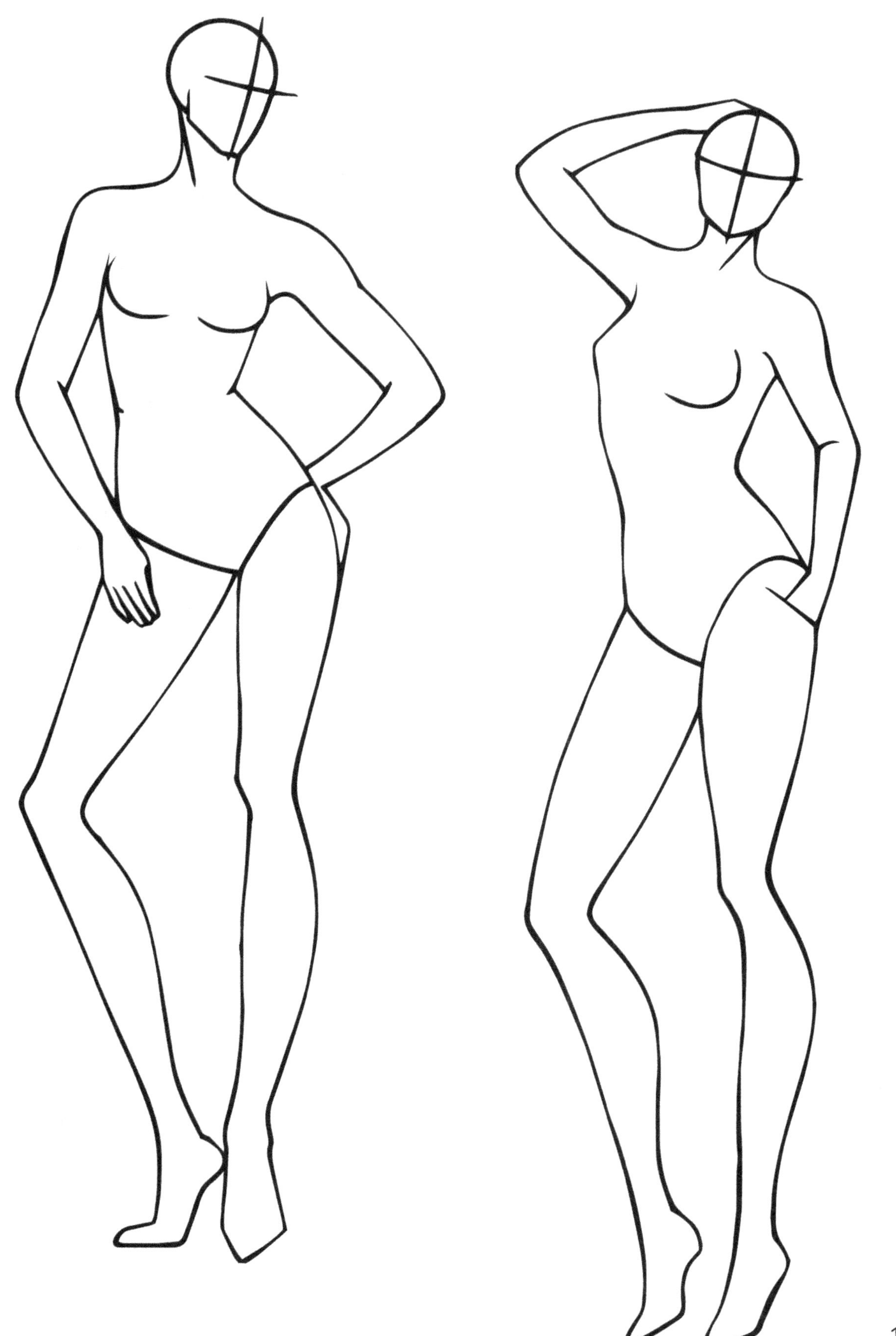

Trends

Inspiration

Textiles

Notes

Details

Swatches

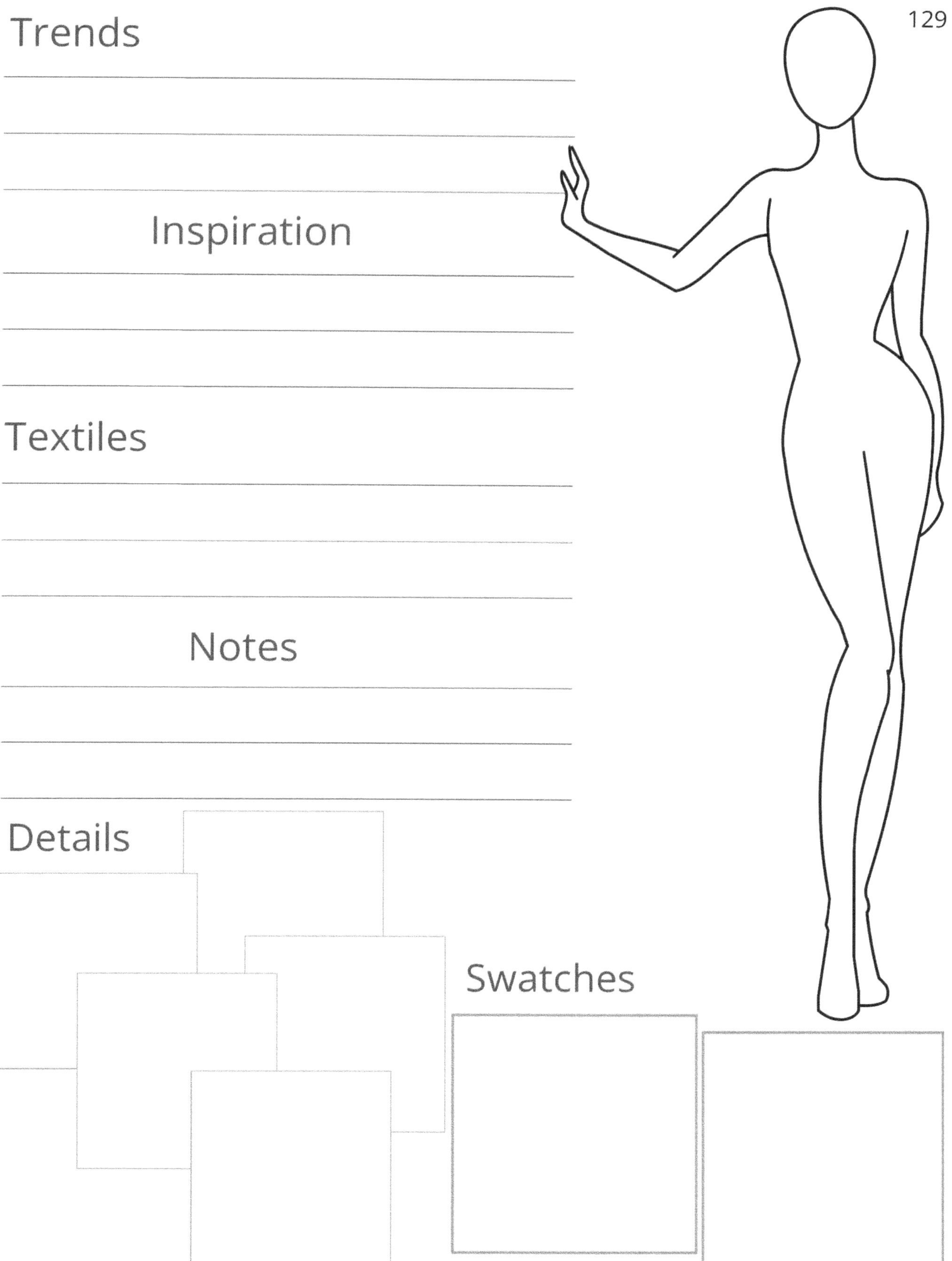

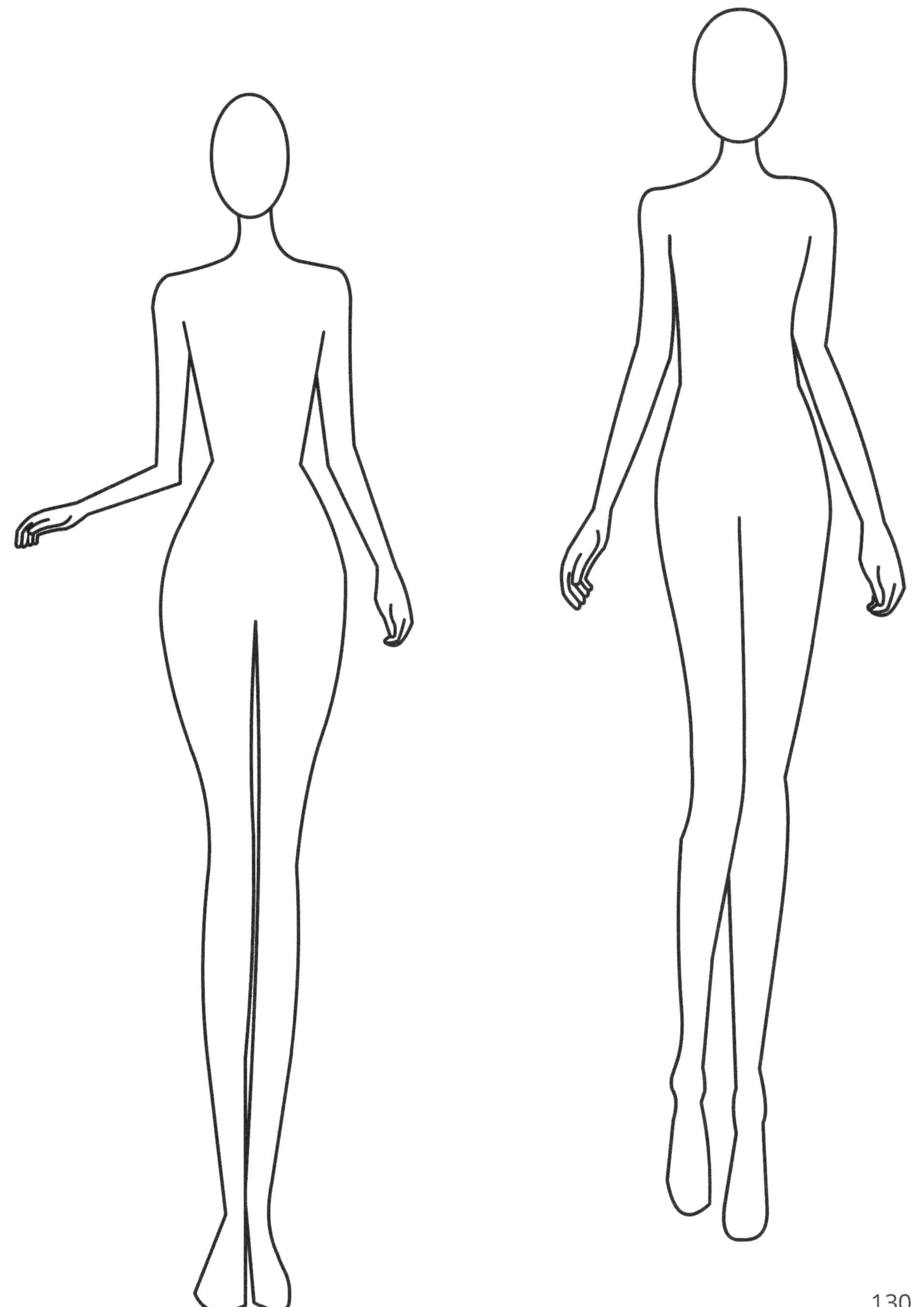

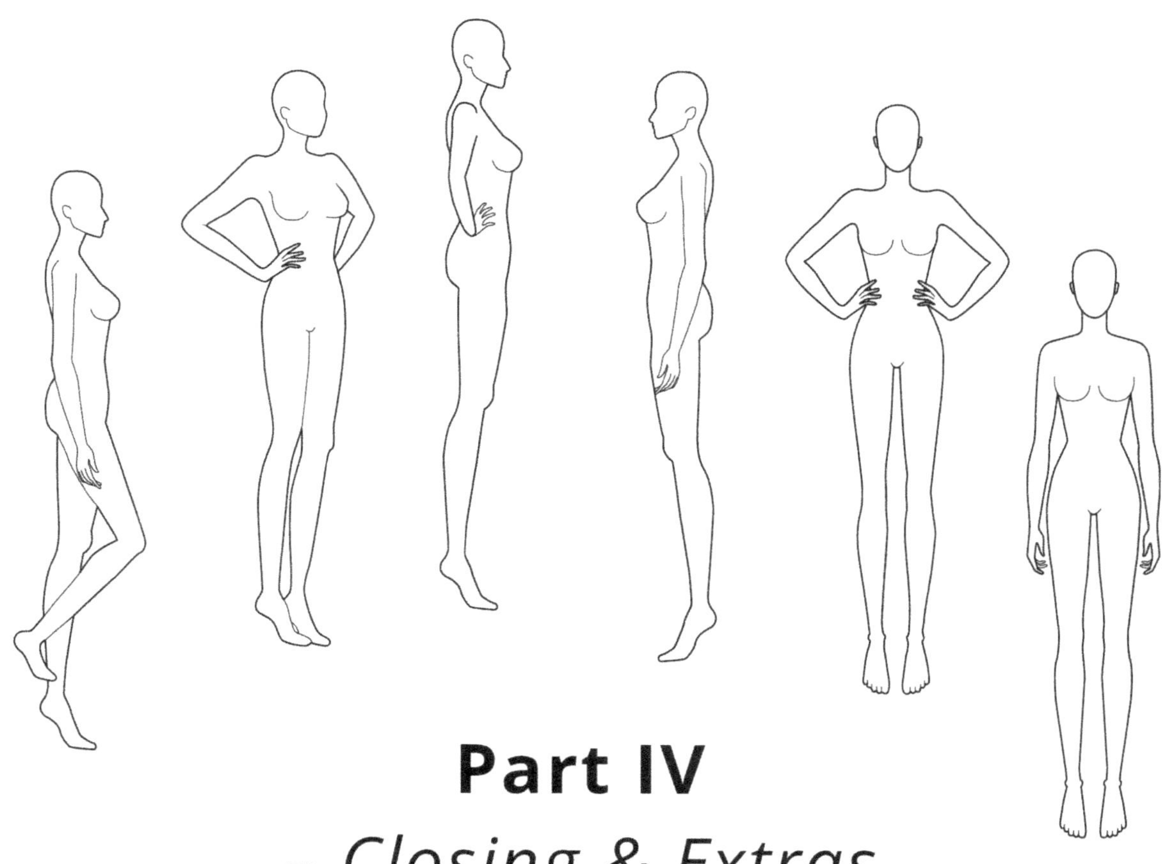

Part IV
– Closing & Extras

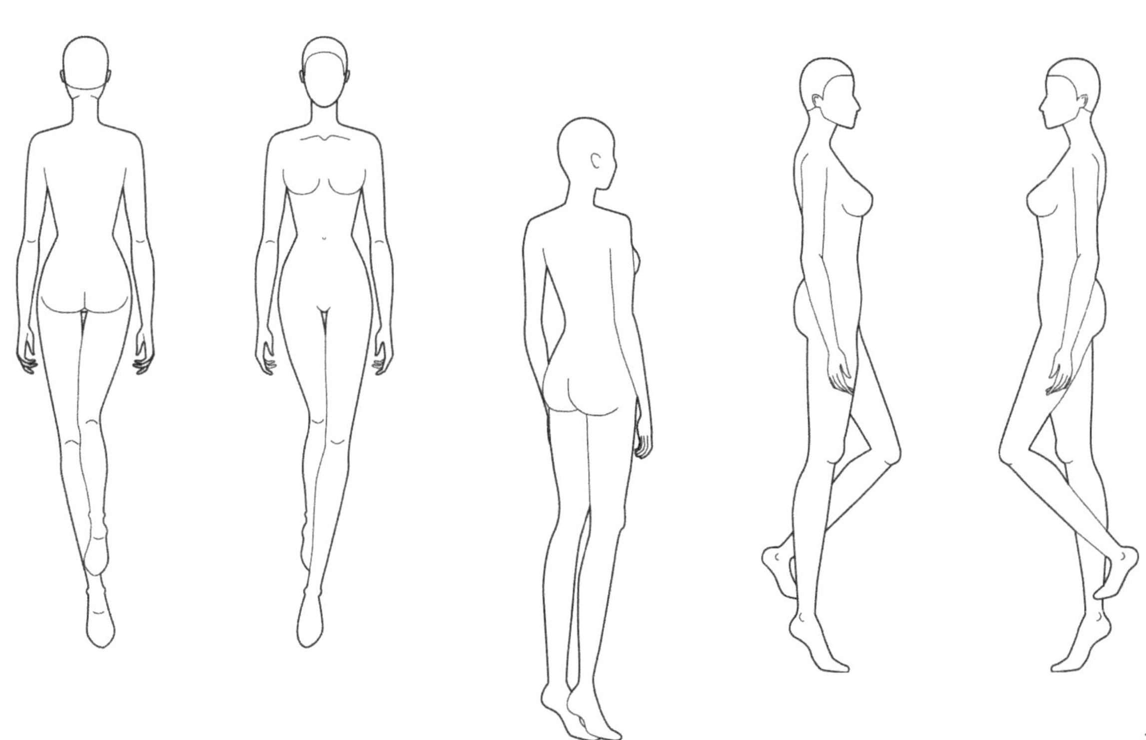

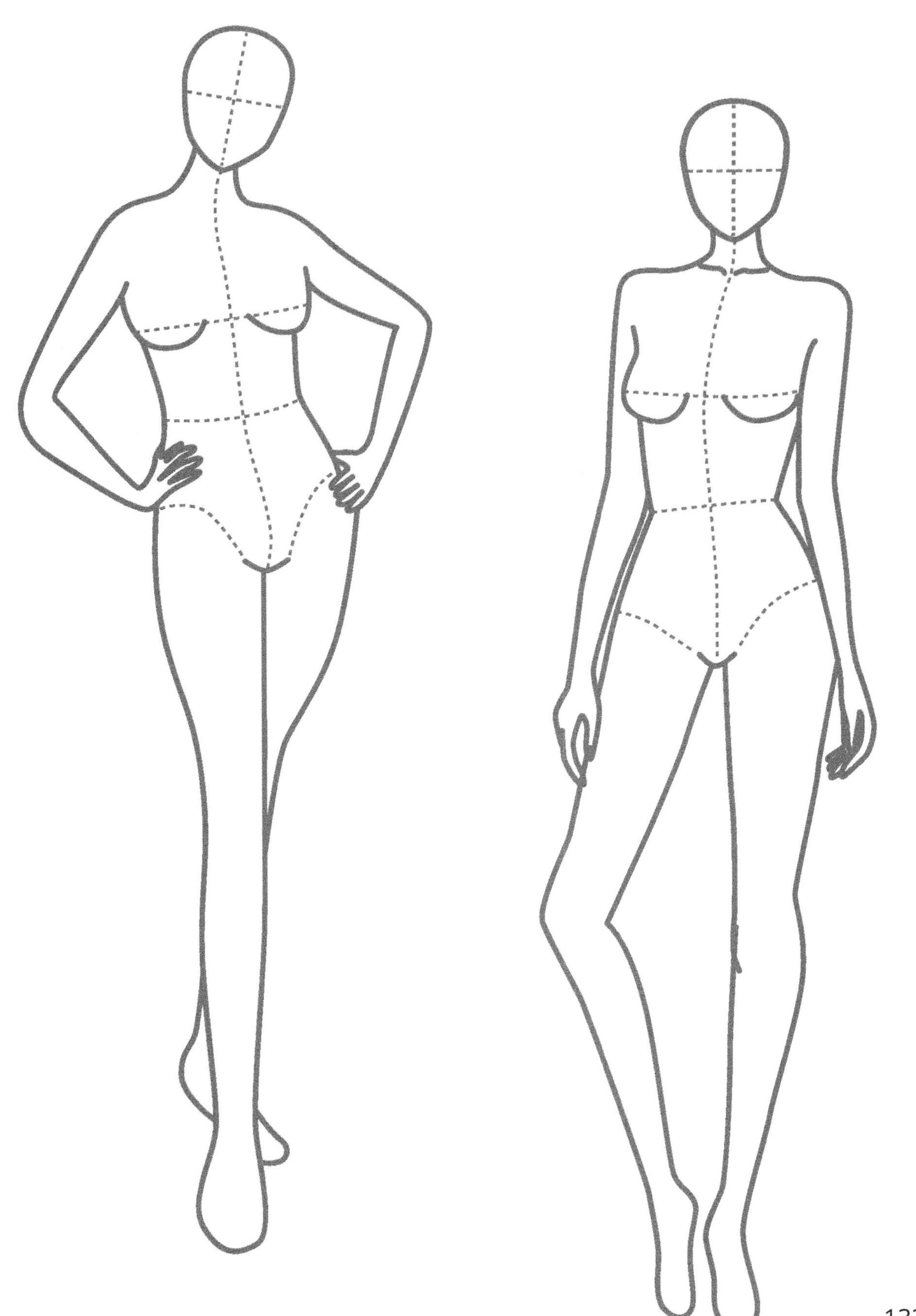

Redesign a Classic Silhouette

Take a timeless silhouette (like a pencil skirt, trench coat, or little black dress) and redesign it three ways. Think about how fabric, color, and details can make a classic piece feel modern and exciting. You could add asymmetry, play with texture, or combine unexpected elements. This challenge helps you break traditional rules while keeping a strong base shape.

Guided Prompts:
- Which classic silhouette did you choose?
- What changes will make it feel more current?
- How would you describe your redesign in one word?

Pro Tip: *"Innovation starts with small twists on familiar shapes."*

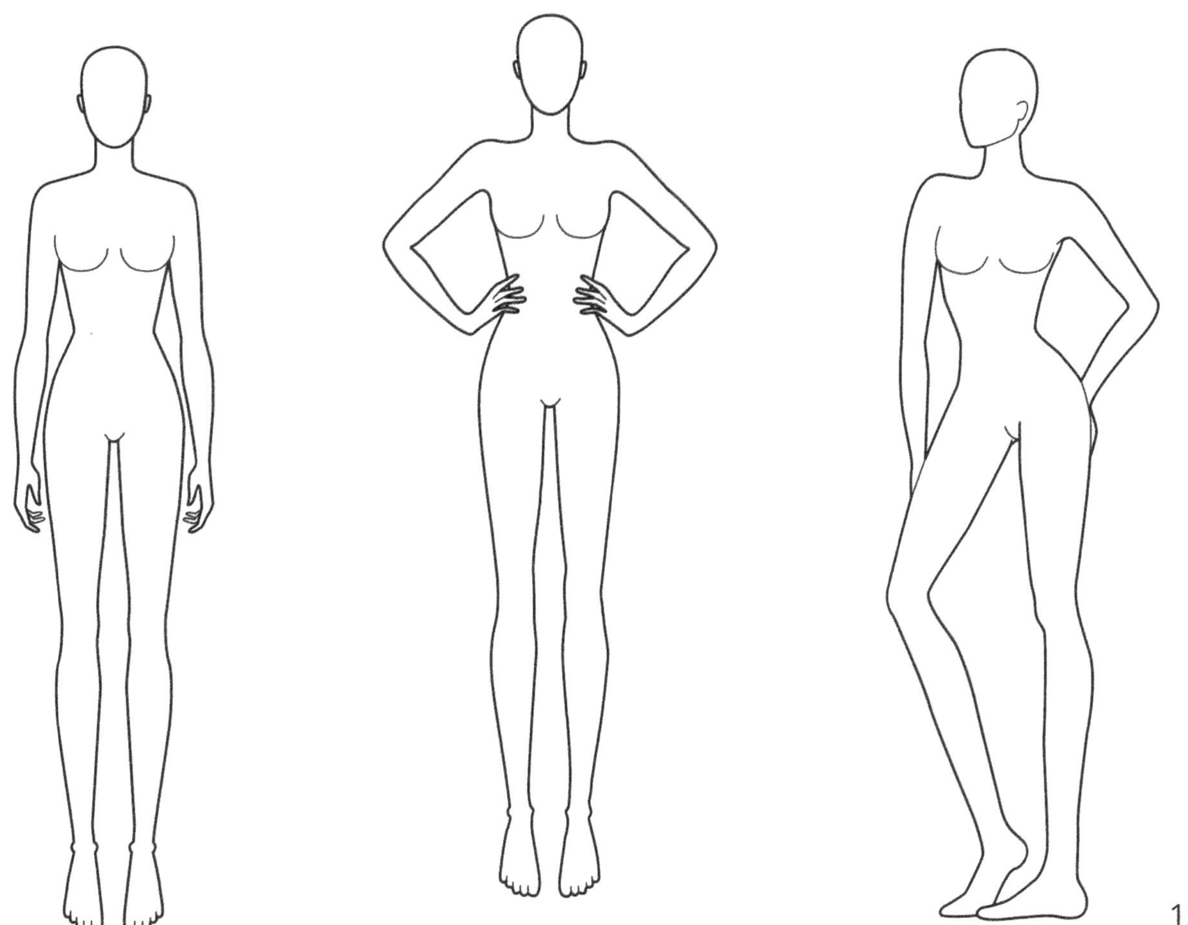

Capsule Wardrobe Challenge

 Design a 5-piece capsule wardrobe that works together. Think tops, bottoms, and layering pieces that can be mixed and matched to create multiple outfits. This exercise helps you focus on cohesion, versatility, and a clear style identity.

Prompts:
- What's the style theme of your capsule? (e.g., minimal chic, boho, edgy)
- Which colors or fabrics dominate?
- How do the pieces combine with each other?

Pro Tip*: "If every piece goes with everything else, you've nailed it."*

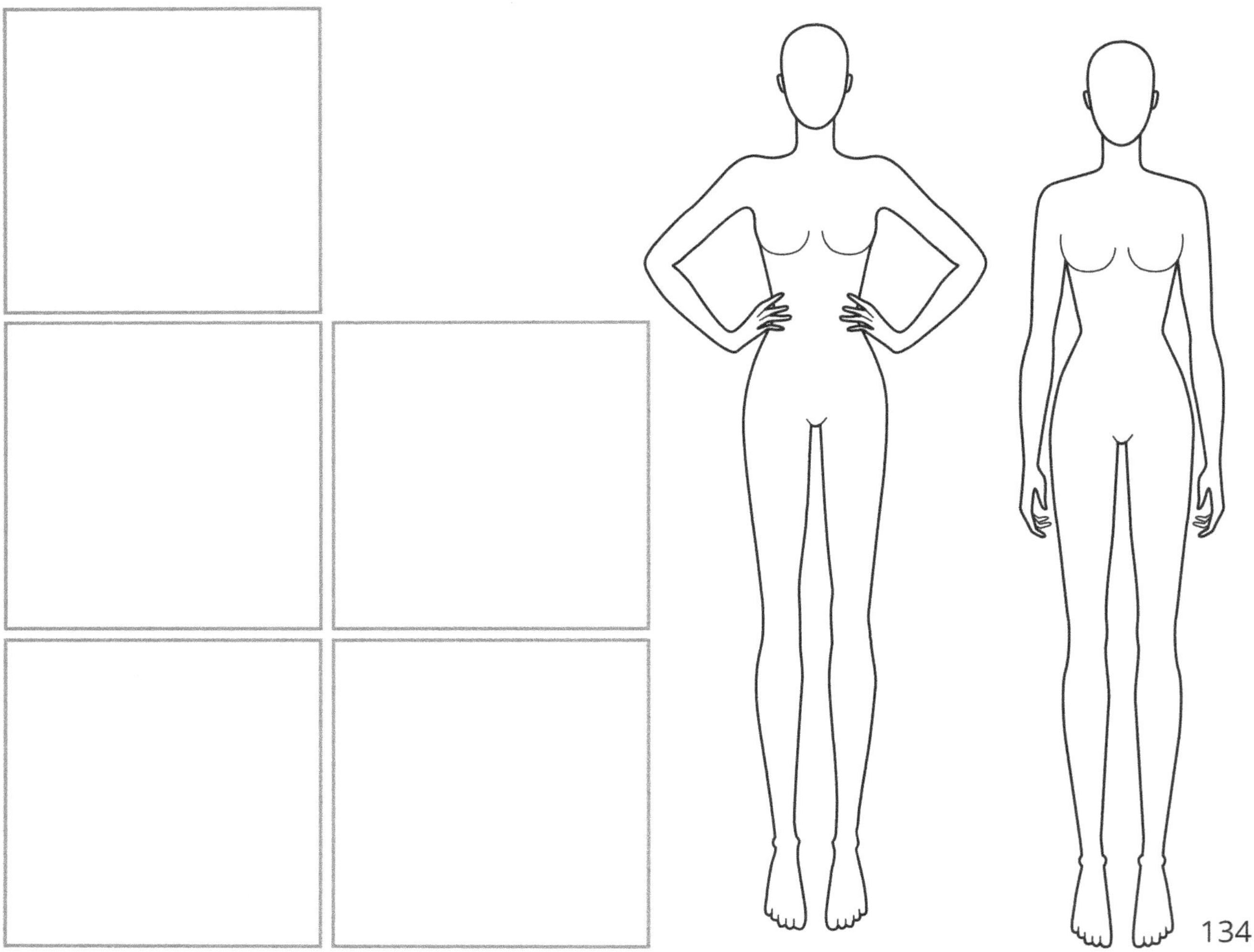

Seasonal Inspiration

Choose a season-spring, summer, autumn, or winter-and design an outfit inspired by its colors, textures, and mood. Think beyond clichés: maybe a winter outfit in unexpected pastels or a summer look in muted earth tones. Let the season guide you but make it yours.

Prompts:
- Which season inspired your outfit?
- Which colors or textures represent it?
- How does this design feel different from typical seasonal looks?

Pro Tip: *"Surprise the viewer by reinterpreting seasonal expectations."*

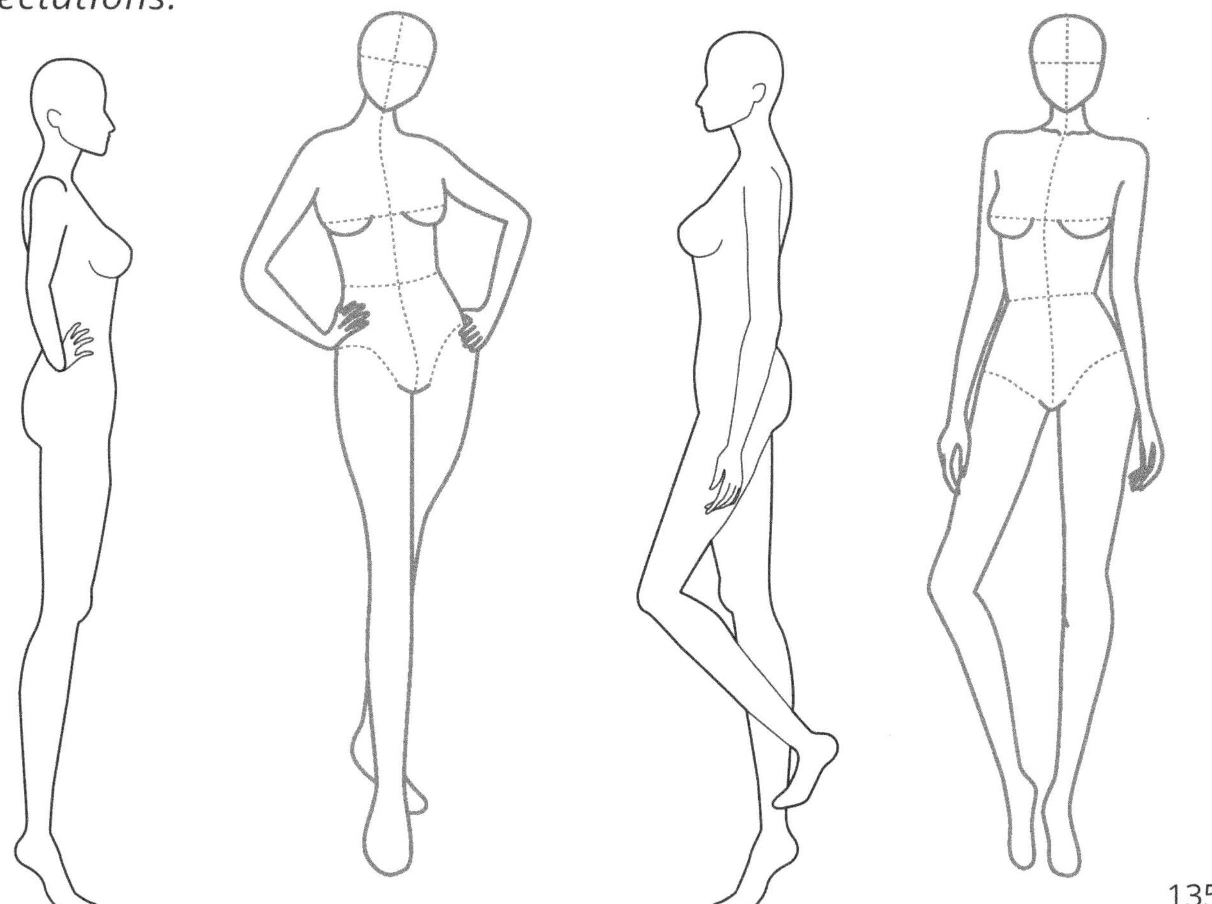

T-shirt Transformation

Take the most basic garment-a plain t-shirt-and reinvent it. Add unique sleeves, alter the neckline, experiment with prints, or turn it into a dress. The challenge: keep the t-shirt recognizable but make it feel like a statement piece.

Prompts:
- What's the mood of your new t-shirt?
- Which element did you change most dramatically?
- Where would someone wear your reinvented piece?

Pro Tip: *"Simplicity is the perfect canvas for bold ideas."*

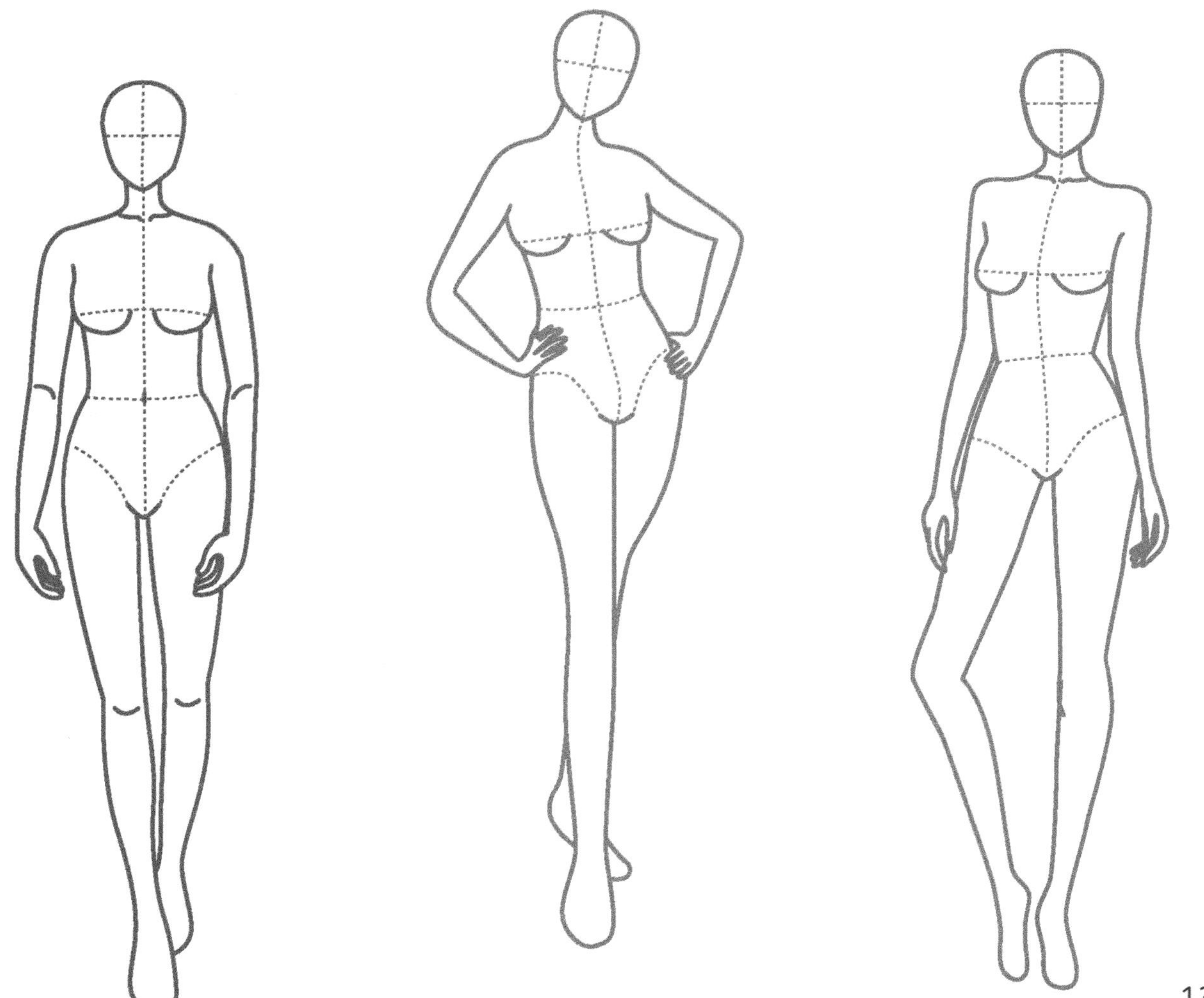

Mix & Match Opposites

Combine two contrasting styles-like sporty & romantic, business & boho, streetwear & luxury-and design an outfit that merges them. This helps you learn how opposites can create new, exciting fashion languages.

Prompts:
- Which two styles are you combining?
- What's the 'bridge' element making them work together?
- Does the outfit lean more toward one style or perfectly balance both?

Pro Tip: *"Fashion's most memorable looks come from contrasts."*

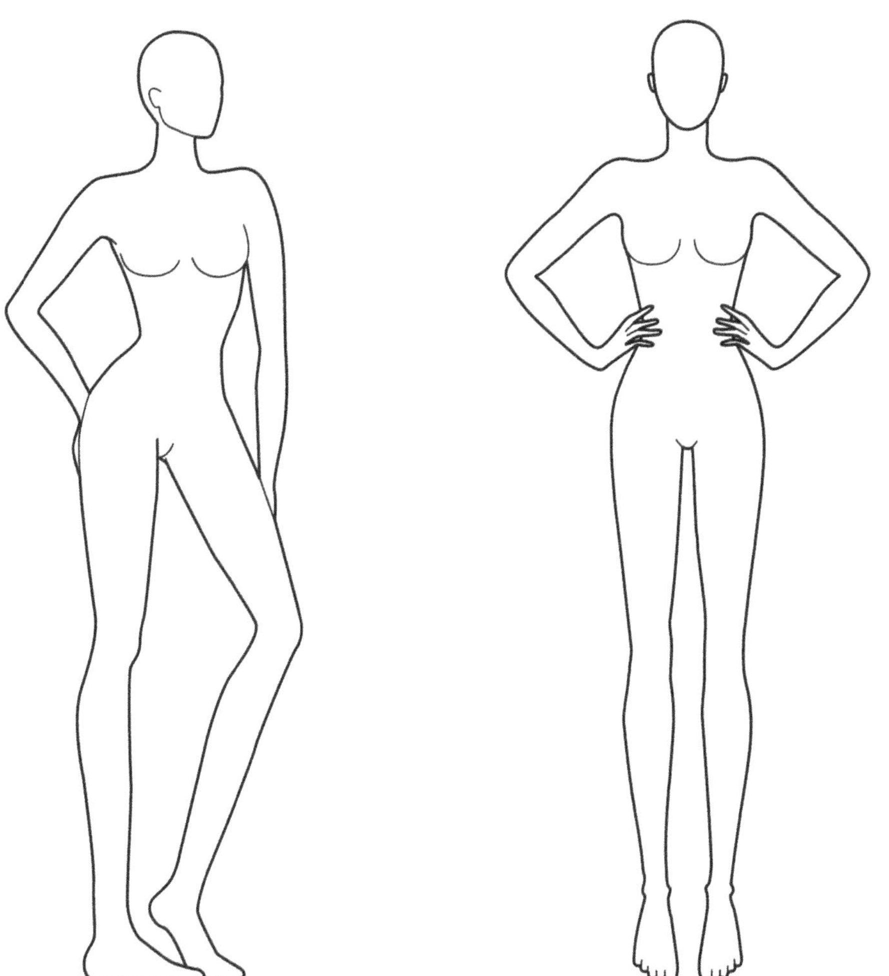

Accessory Focus

 Design a look where accessories are the star. Shoes, bags, hats, jewelry-anything goes. Keep the clothing simple so the accessories shine. This trains your eye to balance focal points in an outfit.

Prompts:
- Which accessory steals the show?
- How do the clothes support the accessory?
- Would this look work without the accessory?

Pro Tip: *"Accessories can turn a basic outfit into a signature style."*

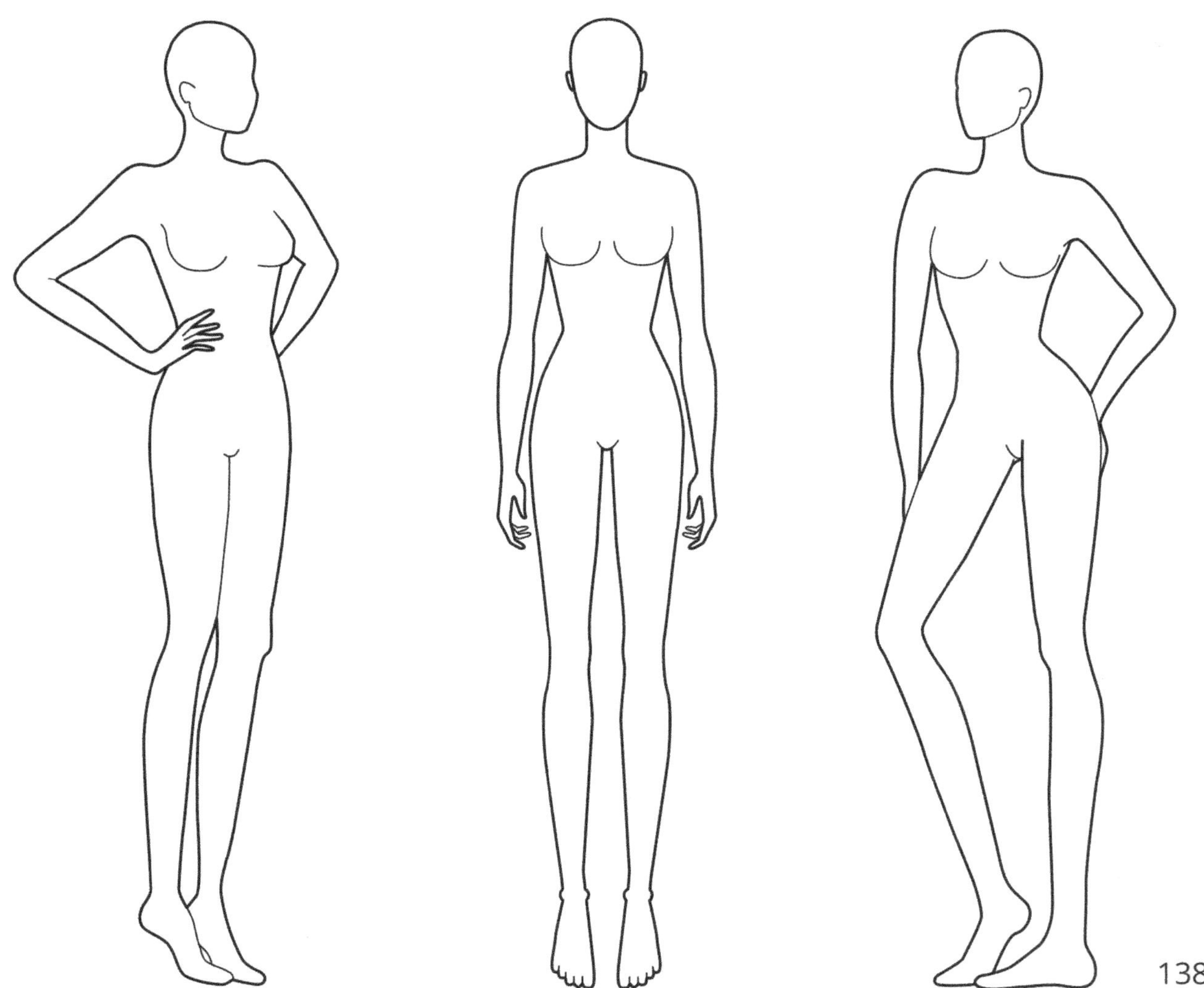

Fashion Through Time

Pick a decade or historical style and modernize it. Maybe Victorian sleeves in streetwear, 1920s beading in a tracksuit, or 90s grunge in luxury fabrics. This exercise teaches you to draw inspiration from history while keeping it fresh.

Prompts:
- Which time period inspired you?
- What's the modern twist you added?
- How does this design fit today's trends?

Pro Tip: *"The future of fashion is built on its past."*

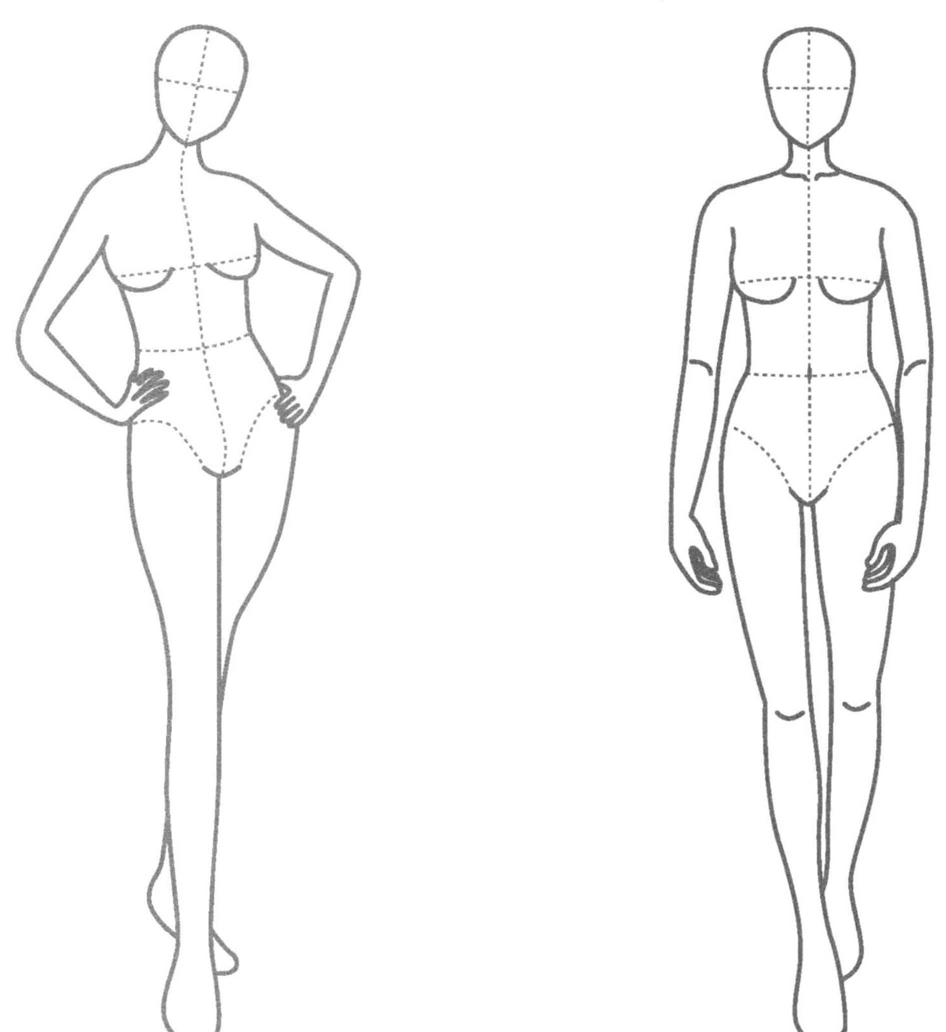

Moodboard to Outfit

Create a mini moodboard and then design an outfit based on it. Gather colors, textures, and images that inspire you, paste or draw them in the space below, and then translate that feeling into a wearable look.

Prompts:
- What's the theme of your moodboard?
- Which elements translated into your design?
- Does the final outfit 'feel' like your board?

Pro Tip: *"A strong concept = a strong collection."*

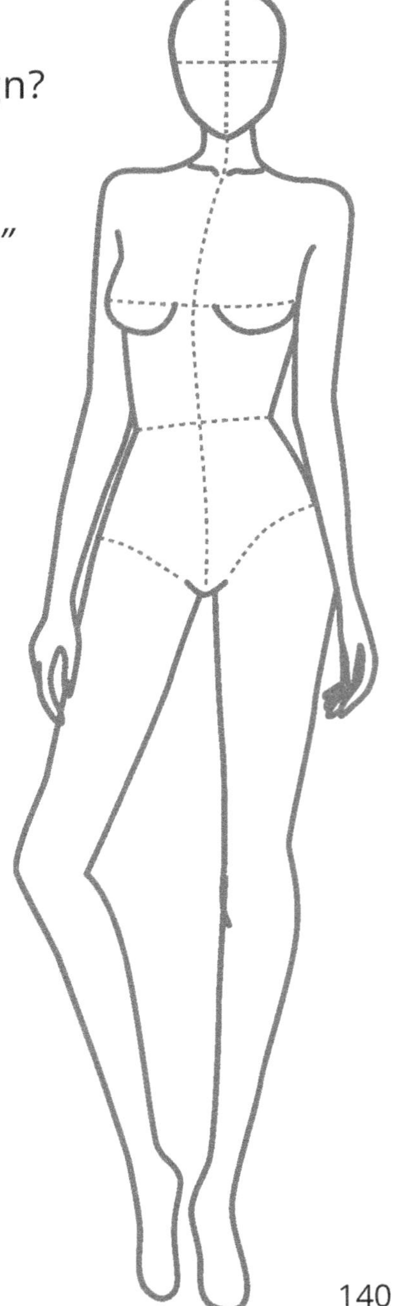

Fashion Designer Checklist

Every designer needs the right tools and essentials. Use this checklist to make sure you're prepared for every sketching session and design project. Tick the boxes as you build your creative toolkit, and feel free to add your own must-haves!

Essentials for Designing

- Sketchbooks & Blank Paper ....
- Fashion Figure Templates ....
- Pencils (HB, 2B, 4B) ....
- Fine Liners & Ink Pens ....
- Erasers & Sharpeners ....
- Rulers & French Curves ....

Color & Textures

- Color Pencils ....
- Markers / Alcohol Markers ....
- Watercolors or Gouache ....
- Fabric Swatches ....
- Texture Samples ....

Tools & Accessories

- Scissors & Cutters ....
- Glue Stick / Tape ....
- Measuring Tape ....
- Pins / Clips ....
- Portfolio Folder ....

Digital Tools (Optional)

- Drawing Tablet ....
- Stylus Pen ....
- Fashion Software (CAD / Sketch Apps) ....

Fabric Research

- Textile Catalogs ....
- Trend Magazines ....
- Moodboard Materials ....

My Favorite Fabrics & Brands

– Space for Notes

This page is just for you! Write down your favorite fabrics, textures, and go-to brands. Think about the materials that inspire you most-whether it's soft silk, sturdy denim, or luxurious velvet.

- My Top 3 Fabrics:
- Fabrics I'd Love to Work With:
- My Go-To Textile Store/Brand:
- Fabric That Represents My Style:
- Dream Material to Use in the Future:

Leave space for notes and small boxes for fabric swatches or taped samples.

My Personal Fashion Journal

A space for your reflections as a designer.

You've reached the final section of this sketchbook-but this is only the beginning of your creative journey. Use this page to capture your thoughts, lessons, and dreams:

- What I've learned so far:
- My favorite designs I created:
- The style that best represents me:
- Next goals as a designer:

"Every sketch is a new possibility. Keep experimenting, keep sketching, keep creating."

____

____

____

____

____

____

____

____

____

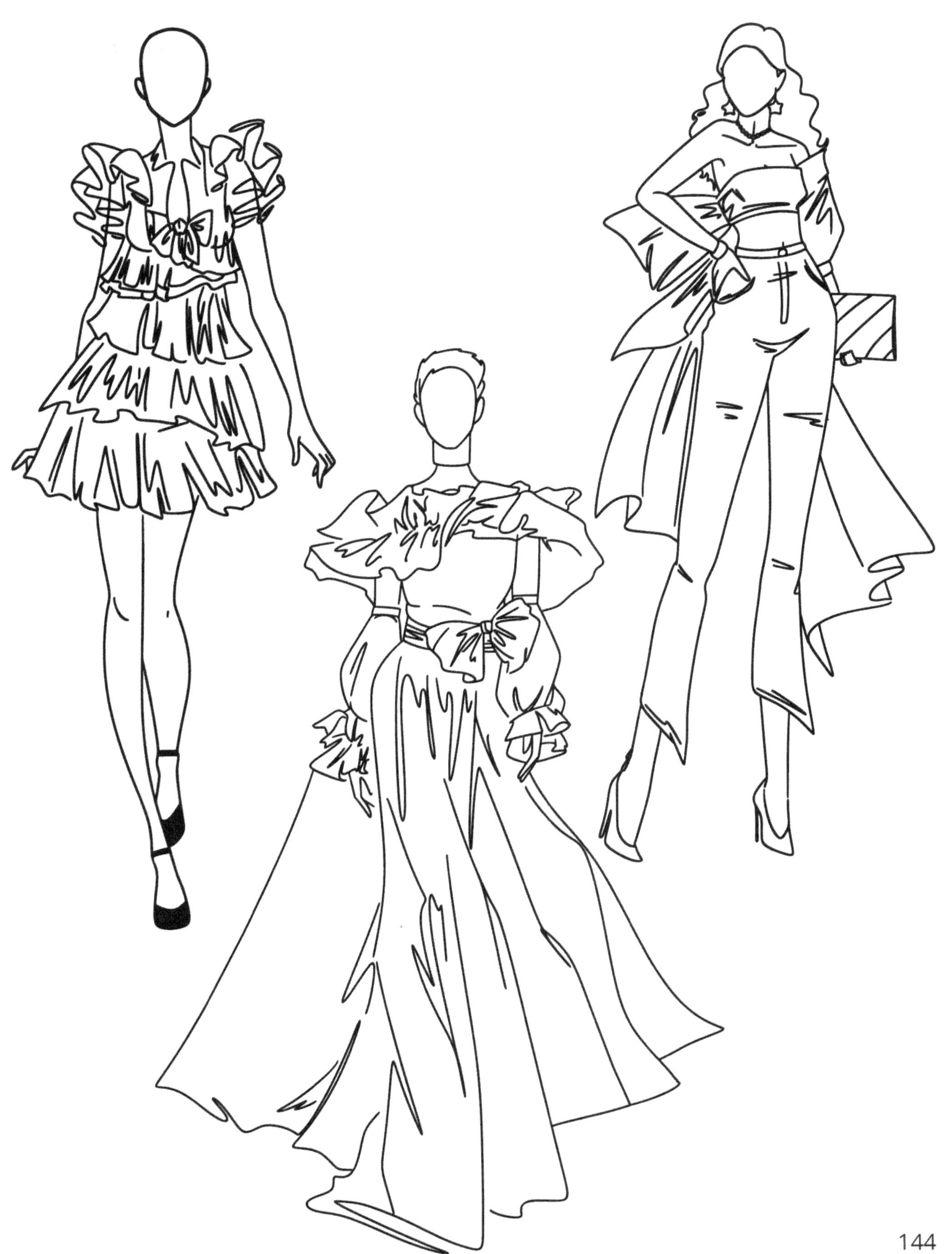

Congratulations!
You Did It!

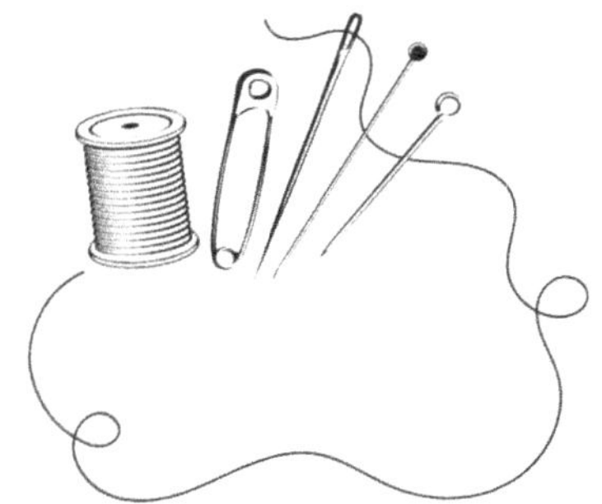

Congratulations, Designer!

You've reached the last pages of this practice book, which means you've invested time, energy, and creativity into developing your vision. Whether you started as a beginner or already had experience, every sketch, idea, and note you added here was a step forward in your journey.

Fashion is more than fabrics and clothes. It's about storytelling, identity, and creativity. Each exercise you completed brought you closer to refining your unique style and building confidence in your craft.

Remember: growth comes with consistency. Keep sketching, exploring, and above all-have fun with your art.

We'd Love to Hear From You!

If this sketchbook inspired you, please take a moment to share your feedback. Your story can help other aspiring designers discover this book and begin their own creative journey.

**Thank you for being part of this adventure!
Keep sketching, keep designing,
and never stop expressing your vision!**

Niky Jadesson

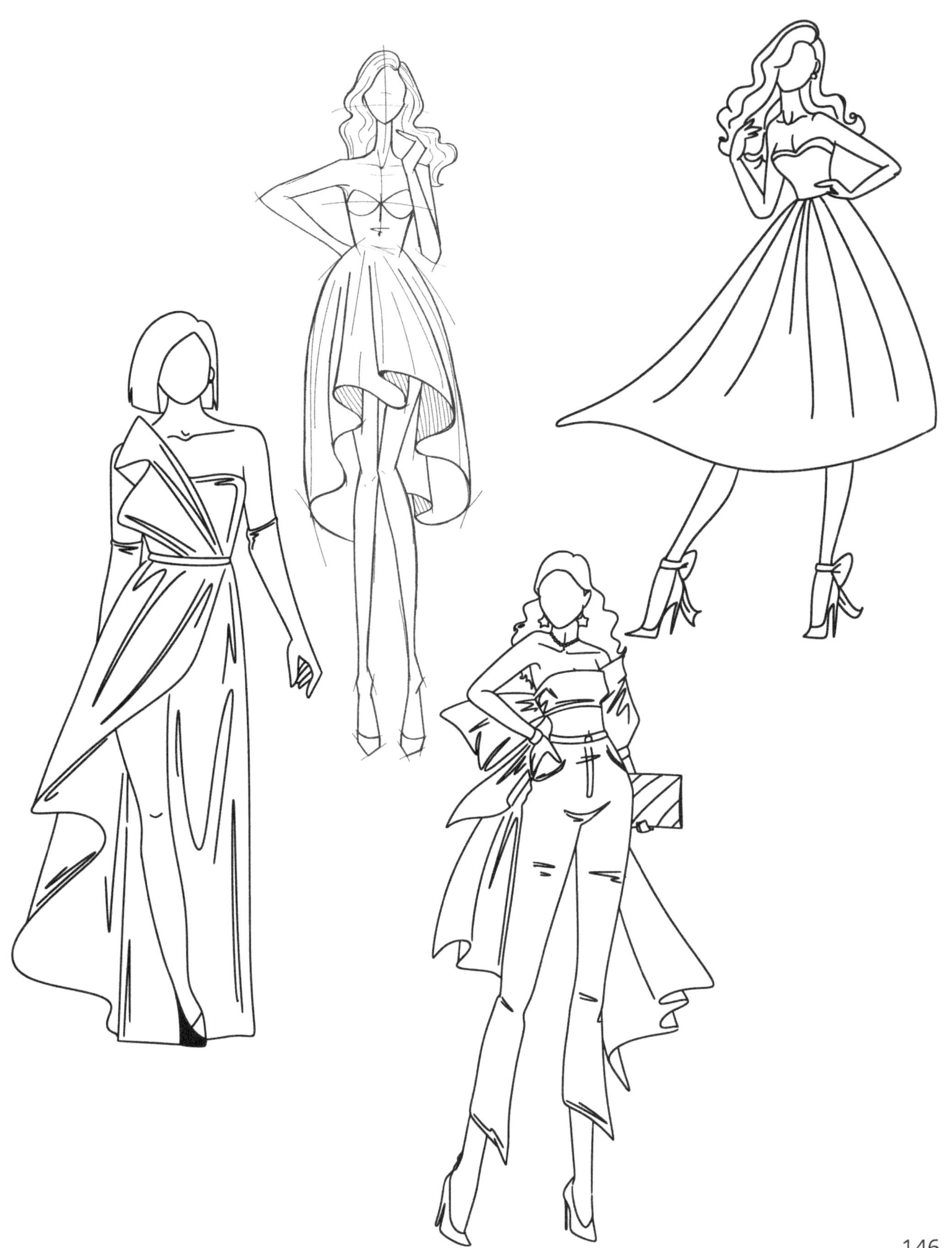

Thank You!

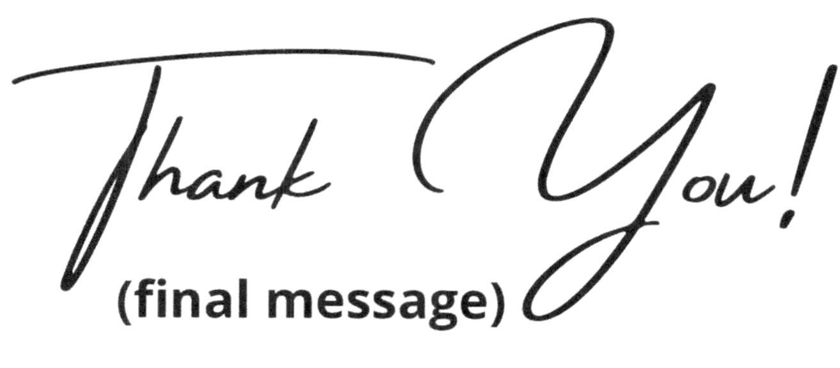

(final message)

Thank You for Being Here!

 We hope you enjoyed this sketchbook and found it inspiring, practical, and fun to use.

Your support means the world to us!

 As an independent publishing project, every review, kind word, or suggestion helps us continue creating more tools for aspiring fashion designers like you.

If you'd like to share feedback, suggestions, or simply say hello, we'd love to hear from you:

 nikyjadesson@gmail.com

You can also discover more design variations of this sketchbook by searching **Niky Jadesson Books.**

 Thank you again for being part of this creative journey-may your artistry continue to shine with every new sketch you bring to life!

Niky Jadesson

Thank You for Choosing This Book!

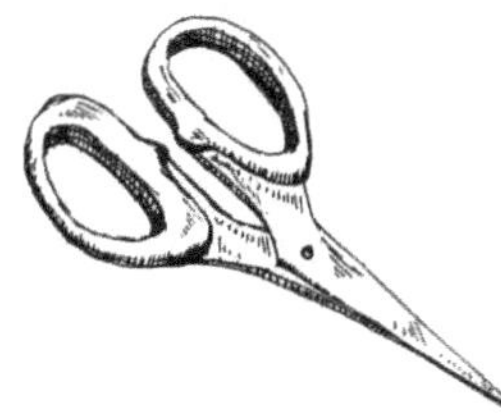 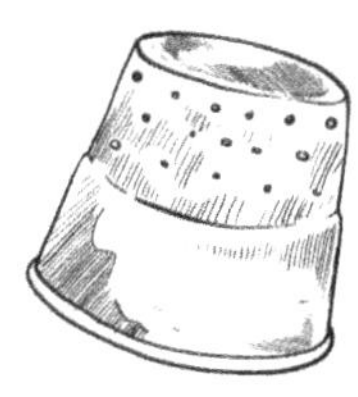 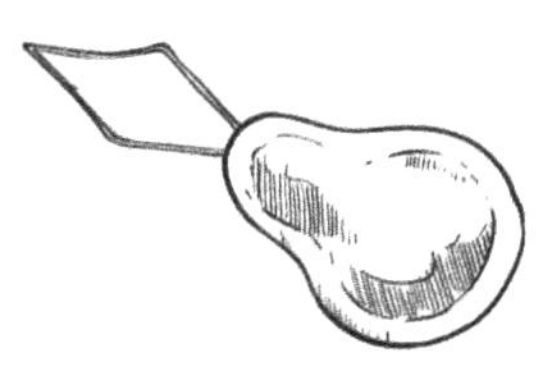 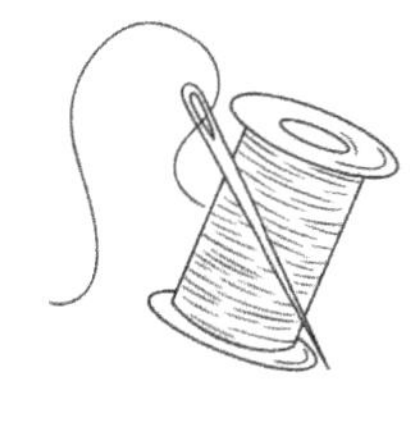

We deeply appreciate the time, effort, and passion you've put into using this sketchbook. Your creativity inspires us to keep making resources that encourage growth, confidence, and self-expression.

If you found this book helpful, your review means so much-it helps other creators discover it and supports our mission to share more.

Want to explore more?
You can find other designs and variations by searching for: **Niky Jadesson Books** online.

Thank you again, and most importantly:

Keep sketching, keep designing, and keep creating!

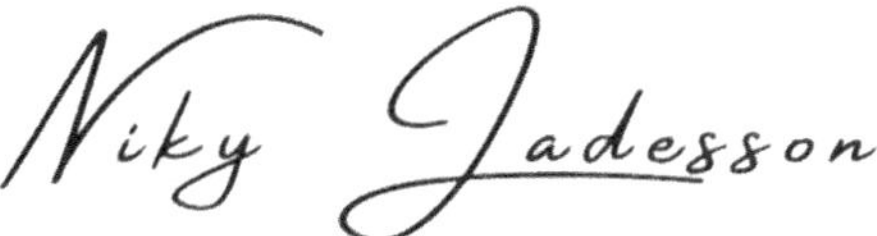

Niky Jadesson

About the Author

Niky Jadesson is a creative author and designer passionate about blending education with imagination.

With a love for both artistry and self-expression, she creates books that help readers explore their creativity, develop new skills, and enjoy the process along the way.

Her inspiration comes from the joy of learning, the beauty of transformation, and the spark of confidence that comes with practice.

When Niky isn't writing or designing new projects, she enjoys nature walks, sipping tea, and brainstorming fresh ways to make learning and creativity more fun.

Her mission is simple: to inspire and empower people to express themselves, one page at a time.

Discover more by searching: **Niky Jadesson Books**

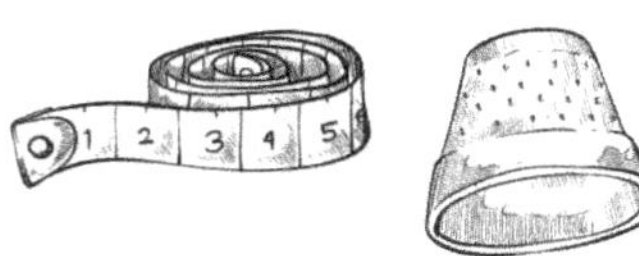# Glossary of Fashion Terms

- **Silhouette** – The overall shape or outline of a garment. It's the first impression a design makes.
- **Pattern** – A template used for cutting fabric pieces before assembling a garment.
- **Drape** – The way fabric falls and moves on a body or mannequin.
- **Seam** – The stitched line where two pieces of fabric are joined.
- **Hemline** – The bottom edge of a garment, usually finished to prevent fraying.
- **Bodice** – The upper section of a garment that covers the torso.
- **Waistline** – The line where the bodice meets the lower garment, defining proportion.
- **Pleat** – A deliberate fold in fabric that adds shape, volume, or design detail.
- **Ruching** – Fabric gathered for decorative texture or shape.
- **Lining** – A secondary fabric layer inside a garment for comfort and polish.
- **Textile** – Any woven, knitted, or manufactured fabric used in fashion.
- **Fiber** – The basic material from which fabrics are made (cotton, wool, silk, polyester, etc.).
- **Couture** – Exclusive, custom-made high fashion pieces, often handcrafted.
- **Ready-to-Wear (RTW)** – Clothing produced in standard sizes and sold in stores.
- **Capsule Wardrobe** – A small, versatile collection of essential pieces designed to mix and match.
- Layering – Styling by combining multiple garments for depth and flexibility.

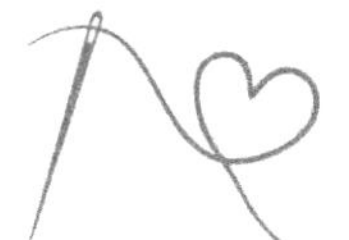 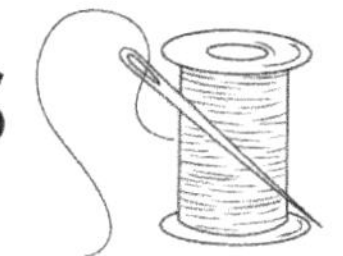

Glossary of Fashion Terms

- **Color Palette** – The selected set of colors used in a collection or outfit.
- **Trend** – A popular style, detail, or garment shape that dominates fashion at a given time.
- **Moodboard** – A visual collage of images, colors, and textures that inspire a design.
- **Dart** – A stitched fold that shapes fabric to fit the body's curves.
- **Yoke** – A shaped panel (often at the shoulders or hips) that supports the rest of the garment.
- **Bias Cut** – Cutting fabric diagonally across the grain for fluid drape and movement.
- **Trim** – Decorative elements like lace, ribbons, or embroidery.
- **Notions** – Small items like zippers, buttons, snaps, or hooks used in garment construction.
- **Sustainable Fashion** – Clothing designed with environmental and ethical responsibility in mind.
- **Fast Fashion** – Mass-produced, inexpensive clothing inspired by current trends but made quickly.
- **Haute Couture** – The highest standard of fashion craftsmanship, often one-of-a-kind.
- **Collection** – A set of coordinated fashion pieces presented by a designer in one season.

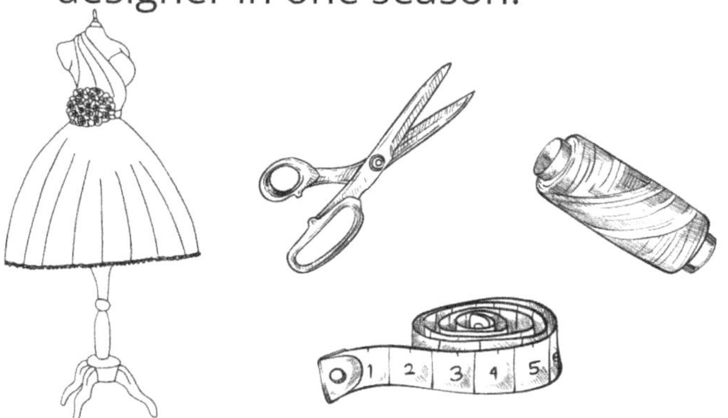

www.ingramcontent.com/pod-product-compliance
Lightning Source LLC
Chambersburg PA
CBHW080449030726
47592CB00011B/3032